Now I lay me down to sleep,
I pray the Lord my soul to keep;
If I should die before I wake,
I pray the Lord my soul to take.

New England Primer, 1737

K. Scott Oliphint is Associate Professor of Apologetics at Westminster Theological Seminary, Philadelphia. He has taught at Westminster since 1991 and has recently published *The Battle Belongs to the Lord* with P&R Publishing.

Sinclair B. Ferguson is Professor of Systematic Theology at Westminster Theological Seminary, Texas Campus, Dallas. Previously he was Minister of St George's Tron Church, Glasgow, Scotland. He is a prolific author and well know conference speaker.

IF I SHOULD DIE BEFORE I WAKE

WHAT'S BEYOND THIS LIFE?

K. SCOTT OLIPHINT
SINCLAIR B. FERGUSON

CHRISTIAN FOCUS

Scripture used in this work, unless indicating otherwise, is taken from the NEW INTERNATIONAL VERSION of the Bible. Copyright © 1973, 1978, 1984 by the International Bible Society. Used by permission of Hodder & Stoughton Ltd. All rights reserved. 'NIV' is a registered trademark of International Bible Society. UK trademark number 1448790.

Scripture marked *Phillips* is taken from *The New Testament in Modern English* by J. B. Phillips.

© K. Scott Oliphint and Sinclair B. Ferguson

ISBN 1-85792-996-9

This edition published in 2004
by
Christian Focus Publications Ltd.,
Geanies House, Fearn, Tain, Ross-shire,
IV20 1TW, Scotland, UK

www.christianfocus.com

First published in 1995
by
Baker Book House Co.,
Grand Rapids, Michigan, USA
Published in the UK in 1995
under the title *Hoping for Heaven*
by
Crossway Books, Leicester, England

Cover design by Alister MacInnes

Printed and bound by Norhaven Paperback A S, Denmark

CONTENTS

To
Peggy and Dorothy
from whose sorrows
love has grown

INTRODUCTION

According to the pollsters, belief in heaven is actually on the increase. Perhaps that is no surprise. After all, large numbers of people still go to church and sing about heaven. Many people probably still say the 200 year-old prayer from which the title of this book comes, asking to get to heaven. Although ours is supposed to be a very secular society, the vast majority of people still seem to believe in heaven and also expect to go there.

Despite heaven's so-called popularity, it is probably true that people give less concentrated thought to it than they do to the location of the annual family vacation. Only when events rudely awaken us are we pressed into asking more serious questions.

Sometimes our children force us to think about death. Apparently they do not share the embarrassment we feel about discussing it. They want to know what happens when a person dies. What do you say when you are asked, 'Where has Grandma gone now?' Whatever private thoughts we may have, we probably respond by saying something like, 'Grandma is in heaven now; she isn't in pain.' We hope, perhaps, that these few words will satisfy young enquiring minds that have not yet discovered the reluctance that adults feel when thinking and talking about death.

The other day one of our children – fascinated by how things happen – asked how caskets are lowered into the ground. Uncluttered by the web of experience and emotion that we adults experience in bereavement, everything seems matter-of-fact to a child. Only later does the subject of death become such an embarrassing taboo that we are reluctant to talk about it. We hope our children's probing questions about life after death will be answered to their satisfaction with a brief reply, 'heaven.' But is this all heaven means to us? Is it merely something that is 'there' for us when we have no other answer to our children's haunting questions? While we moderns regard our forefathers' supposed prudery on the topic of sex with a sense of slightly cynical superiority, would they be astonished by our apparent prudery on the subject of death?

This world seems so real and weighty, and so busy. Heaven seems distant in space and time, unreal in experience – it can wait. Sadly, though many of us believe in heaven, not so many of us seem to know very much about it. No wonder we feel so uncertain, even insecure, when our children innocently probe a little further with their eager and inquisitive questions.

The Christian faith has an amazing amount to say about the life to come. We have written *If I Should Die Before I Wake* to share some of this Christian teaching with people who have unanswered questions or who feel confused, in distress, or anxious.

We know that many secretly experience deep anxiety when they think about death – their own, or that of others. Secret fears lurk deeply in the hearts of even the most apparently composed and successful people.

Perhaps you feel that you know almost nothing about what the Bible teaches about heaven. You may be uncertain about what you have to do to get into heaven. You may not even be sure whether there is anything you can, or even need to do, to get there. You may not even be at all sure that you are going to heaven. You may question, 'Am I good enough? Is it even possible to be sure about something like that?' If you are like most others, you may be reluctant to think about heaven at all because it reminds you of death.

The mental panic that the thought of death creates is probably the greatest single reason we do not think much beyond it. For all its popularity as a final destiny, heaven remains an unpopular topic of conversation.

If I Should Die Before I Wake discusses death and explains why no one really dies of 'natural causes.' It asks the question: 'Why do you expect to get to heaven?' and looks at false and true answers. We hope it will help explain what the Bible has to say about the future and about what heaven is like.

These pages are also about living. Facing death enables us to face life, for assurance about our future in heaven makes an enormous difference to our lives in the present. In the quaint words of the title song of a long-forgotten book of many centuries ago, this is a 'plain man's path-way to heaven.'

We have both experienced the great pastoral privilege of being brought into the very center of families in times of bereavement and sorrow. If you are reading these pages at such a time, we count it a privilege to enter into your life in this way. Seasons of acute grief are not unusually the times to begin the quest to understand biblical teaching. We hope that these pages will bring light and hope at such times, but we also want to encourage Christian living that is marked by a heavenly spirit and an assurance that will transform everything – in times of either sorrow or joy.

Our joint prayer is that *If I Should Die Before I Wake* will help and encourage you.

1

THE END

This morning we saw a car slide smoothly out of the parking lot in the local shopping center. The driver was a beautifully dressed, impeccably groomed woman. She would probably be best described as 'holding on successfully to her middle years.' The car was a gleaming Jaguar. The Pennsylvania plate was obviously personalized. The door closed with the gentlest click. The engine started up almost imperceptibly. The car moved away virtually noiselessly and so gracefully that it was hard not to feel a twinge of jealousy.

'What a car!' We made our way to our own modest automobile parked nearby. Should we be jealous? Only for a second, for the thought came: *But she can drive it only so far; she can't take it with her!*

A moment later, another car pulled out a few parking spaces further down. It was driven by a poorly dressed, elderly man. He looked in his late sixties or early seventies and had the air and appearance of someone who was either retired or perhaps unemployed. His auto had seen better days in a previous decade.

He opened the rusty, battered door of the beaten-up station wagon. The engine revved up noisily. The car stuttered and spluttered as though against its will. Moments later he too was gone. Different thoughts passed through our minds now: *What a heap. Should we feel sorry for him in his apparent poverty?* Then another thought came (and a smile with it): *Well, he doesn't need to take it with him either.* At the end of the day, the rich man (or woman) in the castle and the poor man at the gate will both leave everything behind. At last they will both be equal.

The Great Leveler

Death, we say, is the great leveler, the ultimate equalizer. 'Pale Death with impartial tread beats at the poor man's cottage door and at the palaces of kings,' wrote the Roman poet Horace. Fame, riches, love of family and friends – none of these can protect us against the one great inevitability.

The words 'You can't take it with you' come so easily off our tongues. Sometimes, sadly, they are an expression of our secret jealousy of someone else's material blessings. But they also have deeper significance. One day we will lose control of all that we have. Everything we hold as precious will slip from a lifeless hand. The greatest of all engineering miracles – the human body – will close down completely. We will breathe our last. We will die. 'Anyone can stop a man's life, but no one his death; a thousand doors open on to it,' wrote the Roman author Seneca. 'Nothing can be said to be certain, except death and taxes,' Ben Franklin wryly tells us.

Have you ever sat down and said to yourself, 'I am going to die. What does that mean? What is death? How do I feel about it? How should I think about it and prepare for it? What will happen to me? What is there after death?' Then the thought may cross your mind: *I do not even know where I would begin.* Such moments of honesty should encourage us to do something to remedy that situation.

Death is not only a certainty, it is also a mystery. Medical science continues to explore it, to redefine it, and to try to delay its arrival. Contemporary western society does everything it can to distance itself from its reality. The sick die in hospital beds, not in their own homes; then the mortician plies his craft, and the funeral services are 'beautiful.'

We are all grateful for the help we receive to ease the pain of death. But at times we are tempted to think that there must be an organized strategy at work that only disguises its harsh reality and therefore does not heal us deeply enough. We are protected from staring death in the face and seeing it for what it actually is. There may be some comfort to our jealous spirits in the fact that death is the great leveler; it makes all of us equal. But there is no comfort in what death equals. It equals loss, separation, and sorrow. Therein lies its power to create the deepest and most abiding pain our hearts can experience.

The Ultimate Mystery

One day a person walks up a flight of stairs carrying perhaps 180 pounds of their own weight effortlessly. The next day it takes two people to carry out the lifeless body. What has happened?

We can answer that question in biological ways. Death can be defined as the cessation of the activity of the brain or the heart; bodies simply wear out. One way or another 'death was due to natural causes,' we are told. It just happens. But no one really believes that in their hearts. Or, better, no right-thinking person can accept that without protest. Death is not natural. If it were, would we feel such deep protests in our souls? If it is natural for the bonds of love and friendship we enjoy to be completely severed, why do we feel so angry about it?

The Ugly Intruder

Death is unnatural because it is destructive. It is something that ought not to be. It is deeply wrong. This, at least, is the teaching of the Bible. Its opening chapters make that clear.

God created people to live in this physical world while enjoying spiritual communion with him. God made humans in his image, as a kind of physical representation of himself (Gen. 1:26-27). In a sense people were created to be miniatures of the great and glorious Lord who created all things.

This is why the early chapters of Genesis emphasize certain similarities between God and humans: God has dominion over the entire creation, visible and invisible; humans, in turn, have dominion over the animal kingdom and the earth (Gen. 1:26-30). God created in six days and rested on the seventh; people, in turn, are to be creative in their work in six days and then rest on the seventh (Gen. 2:2-3).

God enjoys communion and fellowship (Gen. 1:26; cf. 3:22). In the biblical story it is clear that in God's being there exist three persons in perfect fellowship with one another; people, in turn, were made 'male and female.' Men and women were meant to sense their likeness to God, to enjoy fellowship and harmony with their Father in heaven and with one another. This gives them a sense of meaning and purpose.

We were thus made for two worlds – one physical and the other spiritual. We have been created to live in and to enjoy harmony with both. Dogs may become good friends, other people may become special friends, but God himself is meant to be our best friend.

God also intended us to grow and mature. This was true physically. The first man was, among other things, a gardener (Gen. 2:15). He was meant to develop muscle tone through the exercise that gardening gave him, quite apart from his guarding and adding to the beauty of the world.

We were also created in such a way that we could develop morally and spiritually by overcoming temptation. Just as we become stronger physically by exercise, so also we become stronger morally and spiritually by choosing to obey, rather than disobey, God's will. This is why the Lord forbade Adam to eat from one of the trees in the garden. If he ate from it, he would die (Gen. 2:17).

Little further explanation is given. The fruit of this tree was not poisonous. It probably looked no different from the fruit growing on other trees. The point of the commandment was to test Adam to see whether he would obey God and trust his wisdom.

If Adam had been obedient, he would have been morally and spiritually strengthened. If the fruit had been poisonous, to refrain from eating it would merely have been common sense. But to refuse to eat the fruit because of God's command – that would have been obedience.

But fail here, God said, and death would be the result: 'dust you are and to dust you will return' (Gen. 3:19). The man and woman, created out of dust in the image of God, would begin to disintegrate and eventually become mere dust again. Glorious creatures of an omnipotent Creator, they would be reduced to earth's minimal-value substance: dust. All that they were created to be would be destroyed. By disobedience they would cut themselves off from fellowship with their life source.

The Great Destroyer

What did the warning that God gave to Adam mean? Did God relent? It certainly appears so. Despite eating the fruit of the tree of knowledge of good and evil, Adam and Eve continued to live.

This is true, at least in one sense. But the rest of the story tells us how 'sin entered the world through one man ... [and] death came to all' (Rom. 5:12). Disintegration and destruction – physical, social, and spiritual – began immediately.

Their God-ward relationship was destroyed. Adam was alienated from God and turned to hide when the Lord came near to him (Gen. 3:8-10).

Their self-ward relationship was destroyed. People were created not only to live in harmony with God, but also at peace with themselves and all that God had made them to be. But now Adam and Eve became dissatisfied. Their consciences, once resting quietly, now rose up to accuse. They were not only guilty of disobedience, but they also *felt guilty*. They became uncomfortable and insecure in God's world (Gen. 3:10).

The marriage relationship was destroyed. Adam was also alienated from Eve. Perversely he blamed God for giving her to him in the first place, and then he blamed her for what was clearly his own disobedience: 'The woman you put here with me – she gave me some fruit from the tree, and I ate it' (Gen. 3:12). The intimacy that they had previously enjoyed, expressed in the simple comment that they 'were both naked, and they felt no shame' (Gen. 2:25), was forever fractured. Now recriminations were the order of the day (Gen. 3:12).

Their creation-ward relationship was destroyed. Adam was alienated from the world of nature. He was meant to have dominion over it, to be its steward and master. Now he would have to labor and sweat to subdue the earth. Ironically, he would eventually be subdued by it. First he would till the soil, but later he would become part of the soil that someone else would till: 'dust you are and to dust you will return' (Gen. 3:17-19).

Family relationships were destroyed. After Adam was driven from Eden, his elder son became the first murderer. Sadly, it was his second son who became the first murder victim (Gen. 4:8).

In time Adam's family tree would develop. The staccato entry on his descendants' gravestones would be repeated time and again: 'then he died' (Gen. 5:5, 8, 11, 14, 17, 20, 27, 31). These words became the universal epitaph. But this relentless onward march of death is highlighted by the fact that there was one exception to it: 'Enoch walked with God; then he was no more, because God took him' (Gen. 5:24). Enoch was the exception that proved the rule. The fact that he did not die served only to underline the new factor that sin brought into the world: all the lesser alienations of our lives eventually produce the most dramatic and tragic alienation of all – physical death.

We usually think of physical death as 'real death.' In some ways, however, physical death is simply the sacrament of death: it is the outward physical emblem of the spiritual reality that is already present. Death involves the disintegration of life and begins as soon as we cut ourselves off from its only true source.

Physical death, then, is the outward expression of this spiritual disintegration. We are like a garment that moths have eaten; it seems to be intact, but it collapses from within at the slightest touch. The threads of the garment lost their strength long ago, and a beautiful garment is reduced to shreds in a moment. A whole process preceded, but the destruction happened in an instant – just like death.

The Minimizer
We have seen that there is nothing natural about death. It is not a native inhabitant of God's order. Paul explains: 'sin *entered* the world through one man, and death *[entered]* through sin ... death *reigned* from the time of Adam...' (Rom. 5:12-14, emphasis added).

What happened? Adam was created to be at home in two worlds – the physical and the spiritual. But now a sinner and cut off from his source, he inevitably experienced disintegration. He no longer felt equally at home with God and with the world. He hid, as though he no longer felt at home in God's presence. He was no longer at home in this world, either – with his wife there were recriminations; in his work there were frustrations; in his family there were estrangements; in his own body there was disintegration. Eventually the impossible and unthinkable would happen: although he was a physical individual, he would undergo traumatic separation from his body. It would lose its life-principle and simply disintegrate.

We are Adam's children. As a result of sin, the life of men and women is minimized, belittled, and finally destroyed.

That is what death does. But there is more.

The Final Paymaster

Death is 'the wages of sin,' says Paul (Rom. 6:23). We deserve it, because we earned it. However unwelcome, it is ours by right. It has already been paid into our account. We cannot avoid it.

When God created man he made him specifically for life-giving fellowship with himself. God's presence was his original natural environment. But Genesis 3 describes how Adam and Eve refused to be content with a life of absolute dependence on God; they wanted to be like God themselves – free and independent of him. Adam and Eve wanted life without limits. Instead of making themselves independent they destroyed themselves. In place of life they experienced death, God's final limit on all our independence.

The greatest and the least of us will be humbled in death. So long as we live and breathe we are scarcely able to take this fact in. The difference between life and death is absolute; it is shattering. Yet we have been so desensitized that we are almost blind to its inevitability. We struggle to avoid contemplating the end of life to which we are daily and irreversibly heading.

The New Testament has a telling way of putting this. It speaks of us being in lifelong bondage through the fear of death (Heb. 2:15). This is the mother of all lesser fears. In fact, it is often obscured by them. But like a mother wart on our skin, if we can be delivered from this mother of fears, all other and lesser warts in our lives will be weakened and we will be transformed.

The message of the gospel is that there is a way of deliverance. It involves facing up to the great fear and its cause. That may well be painful. But it will lead to freedom from the fear of death, joy in living, and peace and assurance about the future.

'Do not be afraid' are Jesus' most frequently spoken words. Be assured that he will be with you as you make your way from the bondage of fear to freedom and assurance.

2

AFTER DEATH

'I have no fear of death.' Sometimes these words are spoken with quiet faith, at other times with a bravado that seeks to mask anxiety or anger in the face of the defeat of life and at the pain that it brings to all who come under its shadow. Death is the final proof that self-interest and self-centeredness cannot triumph because they cannot endure.

There is always a further dimension. It is underlined by the author of the letter to the Hebrews, although his words are etched already in our instincts: 'man is destined to die once, and after that to face judgment' (Heb. 9:27).

Can I face God's judgment of my life with confidence in myself? Surprisingly, large numbers of people believe they can. Many Americans believe that when they die they will pass the scrutiny of God's judgment and enter heaven. Yet most of us will admit that we are rather vague about how God's assessment will be made. What does the New Testament have to say to us?

The most obvious feature of God's judgment is that it is universal in nature; no one will escape it. From the Bible's very first description of God as judge it is clear that the whole world is his courtroom and every man and woman is subject to his judgment. He is 'the Judge of all the earth' (Gen. 18:25).

This is not exclusively an Old Testament teaching. God is 'the judge of all men' (Heb. 12:23). When his judgment is portrayed in the New Testament, all the inhabitants of the earth are subject to it (cf. Matt. 25:32).

The most extensive exposition of God as Judge is found in the vivid judgment scene that Paul portrays in Romans 2:1-16. He stresses its universal nature: 'to each person' (Rom. 2:6, quoting Ps. 62:12). There are no exceptions, as becomes clear later in Romans when the verdict is pronounced and the sentence is given (Rom. 3:9-20).

What are the important things to know about this judgment? Paul gives us the following fundamental principles.

God's Judgment Is True
'God's judgment ... is based on truth [on the reality of the situation]' (Rom. 2:2). Our own assessments of others are always partial and therefore imperfect. At best they approximate the truth. We cannot marshal all the evidence and take all of the circumstances into account. We see the outside, and have, at best, a fragmentary knowledge of the inner dynamics involved in others' actions. We are easily misled and often misinterpret situations.

But God's judgment takes account of the true state of affairs. He is our Creator, and he perfectly understands the norms he has set for human behavior. Since he is faithful to his own nature, his judgment is also rigorously fair. There will be no partiality in his assessment of things. 'God does not show favoritism' (Rom. 2:11). It will not be possible to say, 'Don't you know who I am?' in the expectation that our position in society will guarantee us God's preferential treatment. He will assess us as we really and truly are.

God's Judgment Is Righteous

Paul speaks of the day when God's 'righteous judgment will be revealed' (Rom. 2:5). God's righteousness is his self-integrity. He is absolutely consistent with his own nature, and also with the specific promises he has made to his people. Nothing will lead him to waver from that norm. If he did so, he would be denying himself.

The proof that God's judgment is righteous (and, incidentally, that it is completely impartial) is displayed in the death of Christ. God promised that those who stood before him carrying guilt would be turned away from his presence. Sin separates those who bear it from God (Isa. 59:2). When Jesus 'bore our sins in his body on the tree' (1 Pet. 2:24) no exception was made. God did not spare Jesus, even though he was his own Son (cf. Rom. 8:29). In his righteousness he would not make any exception. When Jesus took the place of guilty humanity, he tasted the deep bitterness of divine abandonment in the depths of his human nature. That is the meaning of his cry of dereliction from the cross:

'My God, my God, why have you forsaken me?' (Matt. 27:46).

Christ's death on the cross, under divine judgment, is the surest possible pledge that God is unwavering in his holy promise that sin will be punished. Even when it is his Son who appears before him bearing guilt, God's judgment is 'according to righteousness.' It is completely impartial.

When Paul tells us that the judgment of God is righteous, he also means that it will accurately reflect our actions. It will fit our crimes. We have a glimpse of that in the Bible's description of the way God already exercises his judgment.

In the first century (as in the present century), those who flaunted God's law took a perverse delight in pointing out that the threatened judgments of God on their so-called sin never actually came. There were no lightning flashes from heaven, no sudden terrible retribution. Either God did not judge, or he simply did not care.

How did the apostles respond to this reasoning? They clarified the two fundamental principles of God's judgment. The first is that God may seem to be slow in fulfilling his threats, but if so, it is because he desires to show mercy and provide time for repentance (2 Pet. 3:9). But more than that, as Paul shows in Romans 1:18-32, the way God often judges is by removing his restraints on human wickedness. If people will not worship him, then let them worship objects that are inferior to themselves. If they insist on giving expression to their sinful desires, then God will give them up to become enslaved to their passions. If they despise the knowledge of God, then God will give them over to 'a depraved mind.' Three times in five verses Paul pronounces these words of divine judgment: 'God gave them over' (Rom. 1:24, 26, 28).

That people feel at liberty to flaunt the laws of God as they do is itself an indication that the judgment of God has already begun. His response to sin is appropriate to our response to him. His judgments are completely righteous in this respect.

God's Judgment Is Individual

God 'will give to each person according to what he has done' (Rom. 2:6; cf. Ps. 62:12; Prov. 24:12). There is no hiding in the safety of the group where God's judgment is concerned: nationality, family, marriage – from all of these relationships we will be singled out for individual assessment by the Lord. *Each one* must give an account of himself or herself (Rom. 14:12).

The New Testament is even more specific about what this means: each one of us will be judged by God on the basis of what we have done. The real significance and effects of what we have done – something even we ourselves cannot possibly assess – will be unraveled. Paul underlines this when he writes that 'we must all appear before the judgment seat of Christ, that each one may receive what is due him for the things done while in the body, whether good or bad' (2 Cor. 5:10). By *all* Paul means everyone; by *we all* he underlines that this includes himself and his fellow believers – all Christians will be judged.

This is a troubling thought for many people. Is it not a denial of Paul's other great conviction that

25

we are justified by grace, not by what we have done? The same teaching is found in other parts of the New Testament (e.g., in Matt. 16:27; Eph. 6:8; 2 Tim. 4:14; 1 Pet. 1:17; Rev. 22:12). But there is no contradiction. Justification is indeed a gift received through faith in Christ. But God's assessment of our justified lives is made on the basis of what we have been and done. This clearly applies to Christians as well. Their lives, forgiven as they are, will be evaluated by God on the basis of what they have done with the grace they have received. That is why Paul appeals to us not to receive the grace of God in vain (2 Cor. 6:1).

God's Judgment Is According to Knowledge

God's judgment will be according to the laws we know and the light we have received. Paul explains this principle very clearly: those who have had the revelation of God's law will be judged by God's law (Rom. 2:12).

It is always illuminating to hear people's reactions to this teaching. Instead of saying with the psalmist 'Lord, if you count my sins, I will never be able to stand in your presence' (Ps. 130:3, authors' paraphrase), we have a tendency to say: 'This is all very well; but what about those who do not have the law?' But can we defend ourselves against God's judgment by pointing out that we are not quite clear about how his justice operates in the case of others? Paul answers this objection almost before we have formulated it: 'All who sin apart from the law will also perish apart from the law' (Rom. 2:12). The fact that a person has never read the Ten Commandments in the Bible does not mean that he or she is free of sin and rebellion against God's law. Even those who do not have the laws that came through Moses know that they are breaking God's law. We were made in his image (Gen. 1:26-27). We still have an instinctive sense of what God requires, however fragmented it may be by our sin: 'the requirements of the law are written on their hearts' (Rom. 2:15).

The truth is that both those who have God's special revelation and those who do not, fail to obey the divine laws they know. That is why Paul solemnly says, 'All who sin apart from the law will also perish apart from the law, and all who sin under the law will be judged by the law' (Rom. 2:12). We may be tempted to respond: 'But surely it is not fair that people will be condemned because they did not receive the special revelation of the Ten Commandments.' If we do, we miss Paul's point: we are condemned because we reject the revelation we ourselves have received, not because we have not received the same revelation as someone else.

Jesus taught that God's judgment will take account of differences of this kind; but notice what implications he draws:

> That servant who knows his master's will and does not get ready or does not do what his master wants will be beaten with many blows. But the one who does not know and does things deserving punishment will be beaten with few blows (Luke 12:47).

The principle that God judges us according to 'the light we have received' does not mean that we can take divine judgment casually. The painful truth is, 'All who sin apart from the law will also perish apart from the law' (Rom. 2:12).

God's Judgment Is Incontrovertible

God's judgment will be confirmed by our consciences. When Paul speaks about God's assessment of our lives he says that our consciences will also serve as witnesses (Rom. 2:15). The basic idea of the word Paul uses for conscience is 'knowledge shared with oneself.' That well expresses what we all experience. Our consciences are not infallible, nor do we possess perfect self-knowledge. Nevertheless, our consciences bear their inward witness to what we believe to be right and true. We may wish that this were not so, but wishful thinking does not of itself silence the voice of conscience.

When God's judgment on your life is pronounced, your conscience will whisper: 'He is absolutely right, you know.' Notice that Paul says this will be true even of the most depraved people: they cannot fully or finally obliterate the witness of their consciences against them. They may try to silence conscience now. But they will not be able to do so at the final judgment. At the end, God will speak and conscience will agree with him. Every mouth will be 'silenced' (Rom. 3:19). No conscience will dare to enter a plea of 'not guilty.' All our protestations will be silenced.

Nothing Is Hidden from God's Judgment

God's judgment will reach into the secrets of our hearts. The day of reckoning is 'the day when God will judge men's secrets through Jesus Christ, as my gospel declares,' says Paul (Rom. 2:16).

The most sobering portrayal of this is found not in the vivid judgment scenes of the great works of art but in the pages of the book of Revelation, from which many artists have drawn inspiration.

> Then I saw a great white throne and him who was seated on it. Earth and sky fled from his presence, and there was no place for them. And I saw the dead, great and small, standing before the throne, and books were opened. Another book was opened, which is the book of life. The dead were judged according to what they had done as recorded in the books (Rev. 20:11-12).

On that day God will 'bring to light what is hidden in darkness and will expose the motives of men's hearts' (1 Cor. 4:5). Not merely acts, or plans, or thoughts will be exposed; even motives that we cannot now detect in ourselves will be unveiled. Paul indicates in this context that he himself cannot accurately assess his own motives, but God can and will.

Our motives are at best mixed, and sometimes even hidden from us; we do not really know and understand ourselves. On the day of judgment, however, the motives that ruled our lives, determined our plans, and came to expression in our words and deeds, will be uncovered. What lay behind our careless comments and incidental acts will become clear (Matt. 12:35-7; 25:31-46). Unmasked we will stand before God's all-penetrating gaze.

'I have nothing to hide,' we say. But to say this is to reveal superficial self-knowledge. We do not even know ourselves well enough to realize how little we understand ourselves. Nothing is more unnerving than to discover the truth about ourselves. Except, perhaps, to discover it too late.

For some the distasteful thing about the idea of a day of judgment is the thought that God might reveal the truth about them to others. How embarrassing! But that feeling indicates how out of focus our thinking about the deep seriousness of God's judgment is. Even if the Bible did teach that, it would be a relatively minor matter. The really sobering feature of God's judgment is that he, the great Knower of the Heart (Heb. 4:12-13), the Infinite Cardiologist, will show us the truth about ourselves. That will be the most devastating discovery of all.

Christ Is the Judge

God's judgment will be in the hands of Jesus Christ. 'God will judge men's secrets through Jesus Christ,' says Paul (Rom. 2:16). This is not an idea Paul invented. He is echoing Jesus' teaching about himself as the Son of Man (his favorite way of describing himself): 'The Father ... has given him authority to judge' (John 5:26-27). And this is confirmed by other statements (see Matt. 7:21; 25:31-33; Acts 10:42; 17:31; 2 Cor. 5:10; 2 Thess. 1:7-8; 2 Tim. 4:1).

Why is it so significant that Jesus Christ, whom the New Testament portrays as God incarnate, is the Judge? It means that we can never appeal to the difference between God and ourselves and say, 'How can you judge when you do not know the realities of human experience?' We cannot say: 'You do not know; you have no experience; you were never tempted as

I was; you did not suffer what I did.' Because he is the incarnate Son, he knows. He was tempted; he suffered.

In the presence of the One who was tempted, but conquered, who was crucified, yet remained obedient to his Father, our self-justification of sin and failure seems hollow indeed. Because he shares our human nature Christ possesses perfect knowledge of the human condition, and in his divine nature he has perfect knowledge of our hearts. His judgment will be perfectly just, infallibly accurate. On the basis of his judgment men and women will be sent either to heaven or to hell.

If heaven is what we all desire, the greatest mistake we could make would be not to know what God has revealed about the way in which he will assess our lives.

Now we know.

Can we still get to heaven?

3

THE WAY TO HEAVEN

Belief in heaven is actually on the increase. A 1990 poll indicates that 78 percent of Americans believe in a place called heaven, compared to 72 percent in 1952. Not only do the majority of people believe in heaven, but the same percentage of people also believe they have a 'good-to-excellent' chance of going there. Such statistics confirm that the overwhelming majority of Americans want and expect a life of bliss after death. There may be different opinions on what heaven is like, but there is no mistaking the fact that heaven is seen, at the very least, as highly desirable.

What could be the reasons for such confidence and hope? One reason is probably the fact that we feel we deserve something better than our present life offers. This conviction seems to be deeply ingrained in people. We vividly remember the confidence with which one particular woman we met responded to the question: 'What will you say to God when you die if he asks you why he should let you into heaven?' Immediately she said, 'Because I deserve it!' Experience suggests that most decent people would probably respond in the same or some similar way.

The more complicated life becomes, the more we tend to cling to something that will help us rise above it all. The television commercial where the overly stressed mother cries out to her bath soap, 'Take me away!' reflects the panic we all feel from time to time in our modern society. Perhaps the popularity of belief in heaven relates to that cry – heaven is the final place to escape.

There is, however, something rather curious about this overwhelming belief in heaven. Despite what the polls tell us – that the vast majority of people are still believers in heaven – most of us seem to be practical unbelievers. Education no longer has as its goal the glory of God. Personal convictions have been reduced simply to what will work best. ('If that works for you, that's great. It doesn't work for me.') The home is no longer seen as the sphere in which both children and parents are schooled for eternity. We live as though this world is all there is. The difference that our belief in heaven makes to our lives is minimal.

It is curious, then, that belief in heaven has statistically increased in our otherwise earth-bound environment – a belief that is glaringly inconsistent with the prevailing secular mindset that seeks explanations for life's mysteries on a horizontal rather than a vertical plane. Could it be that once we place ourselves at the center of the world and make ourselves the 'measure of all things,' we hold on to the otherwise outmoded belief in heaven because we feel we simply must live forever? It would be ironic if a worldview designed to destroy any thought of life beyond this one actually tended to preserve the very thing it sought to erase!

We learn from Scripture that unbelieving thought does produce such ironies and contradictions: 'Although they claimed to be wise, they became fools and exchanged the glory of the immortal God for images made to look like mortal man' (Rom. 1:22-23). People, at the center of their universe, believe that of themselves and by themselves they have emerged from the slime: that despite their origins, they are indestructible, even beyond the grave. In any event, in our modern, rights-oriented society, it has become unthinkable that we might not go to heaven when we die. The very idea is almost an affront to our constitutional and democratic ideas of life, liberty, and the pursuit of happiness.

Reasons for Confidence
But there are also other explanations for such confidence. Every religion (except the Christian faith, as we shall see) teaches in one form or another that people can earn the right to get to heaven. When asked why they expect to go to heaven after death, most people answer in such terms as: 'Because of what I have been and done.' There are two reasons why they may feel this way.

The first is the belief that their 'status' will get them to heaven. Status might include the fact that they are Americans, they belong to a nation with deep Christian influences in its traditions, or that their families have been connected with the church for generations (whether it be Episcopalian or Roman Catholic,

Baptist or Presbyterian). After all, 'membership has its privileges' (as the credit-card commercial puts it). Since their credit is good in human society, it will surely be good in the heavenly society, especially since God is love.

This idea, that there is a kind of group-plan arrangement that secures our place in heaven, is not new. Jesus met it in his day. On one occasion, the Pharisees used their own form of the membership-has-its-privileges argument: 'Abraham is our father ... We are not illegitimate children ... The only Father we have is God himself' (John 8:39, 41). They were convinced that their natural relationship with Abraham guaranteed their membership in the family of God. They were born to go to heaven, or so they thought.

Jesus' response was devastating:

If God were your Father, you would love me, for I came from God and now am here. I have not come on my own; but he sent me. Why is my language not clear to you? Because you are unable to hear what I say. You belong to your father, the devil, and you want to carry out your father's desire ... The reason you do not hear is that you do not belong to God (John 8:42-44, 47).

According to Jesus, the privileges of belonging to the family of God, either here and now on earth or there and then in heaven, require more than membership in a natural family, a church, or a country.

The second reason why people tend to rely on their own efforts relates more to the way we think of ourselves as individuals. Heaven is our right because of what we have done. We get to heaven the old-fashioned way: we earn it. However modestly we express it, we feel we deserve it.

Perhaps only some of us would express it quite this boldly, yet most of us naturally feel that we are good enough and better than most. Polls indicate that the vast majority of people believe themselves to be better-than-average car drivers, even though it is not actually possible for most people to be better than average. We also feel we are better-than-average people. If there is an entry test, we have secured a good enough grade to pass. But what if neither our driving nor our living skills are better than average?

We all have our own version of this attitude. We have been sincere. We have tried to be decent people. We feel that on the whole we have done more good than harm. Surely heaven awaits us in the end. In addition, when we compare ourselves with others we believe there are many who are worse than we are (the state of prisons have an overcrowding problem, after all), or certainly less respectable than we are. How could we possibly miss heaven? We certainly have done nothing to deserve exclusion.

An Offensive Exclusiveness

Does it surprise you to learn that another poll indicates that the most offensive teaching of the Christian faith is that Jesus Christ is the only way to the Father and therefore to heaven? Why do people find this so offensive? Do they simply forget themselves? Does it just slip their minds that these are the words of Jesus himself (John 14:6)? No, it is offensive to people because it destroys their assumption that they are already on the road to heaven. It questions whether they have a good-to-excellent chance of arriving there. It destroys their Sinatra-esque confidence ('I did it my way') or their Beatles-like assurance ('I'll get by with a little help from my friends').

It is a pity that we do not have more detailed statistics. If we did, they would probably indicate that many of those who feel assured of their going to heaven find offensive the idea that heaven can be gained only through faith in Christ.

Ultimately, however, the reason for the offensiveness of Christ's claim is our reluctance to admit our often offensiveness before God. In this connection the Bible makes two important points:

First, God is holy. The holiness of God includes his absolute purity. But even more, it refers to his exalted and majestic character as the Creator. God's holiness marks everything that he is and does. His love is a holy love. His mercy is a holy mercy. His grace is a holy grace. His wrath is a holy wrath. His jealousy is a holy jealousy. That is why he is worthy to be worshiped, served, and adored by his creatures.

As holy, God is distanced from everything he has made. He is never limited by, or identified with, anything in his creation. He is transcendent, separate from his creation. This separation is itself an indication of his absolute holiness. But God also hates and distances himself from our sin: his eyes are too pure to look on it (Hab. 1:13).

Second, we are unholy. We have been born in a condition that is repugnant to the holy God of heaven.

We are not fit to enter his presence. From the beginning of our lives we have been hostile to God. This was the terrible discovery King David made when he realized that his sin was entwined in the earliest and deepest strands of his being: 'Surely I was sinful at birth, sinful from the time my mother conceived me' (Ps. 51:5). We are never naturally acceptable before God.

The depth of our unholiness reaches far beyond what we have done. It reaches into the secret recesses of our hearts, going back in our personal history as far as our conception. We therefore begin our existence as unacceptable and unworthy rebels against a holy God.

The truth is that the other world of which the Bible speaks is the world where the holy God dwells. And it is just because he dwells there that we, in our sins, cannot. In fact, no question penetrates more deeply into our real interest in heaven than this one: if heaven is a world filled with holiness, do I really want to be there?

There is no natural pathway between this life and heavenly bliss: only an infinite chasm. Frederick W. Faber saw this with great clarity when he was moved to write:

> The spirits that surround thy throne
> May bear the burning bliss;
> But that is surely theirs alone,
> Since they have never, never known
> A fallen world like this.
> O how shall I, whose native sphere
> Is dark, whose mind is dim,
> Before the Ineffable appear,

And on my naked spirit bear
The uncreated beam?

The idea that heaven is naturally our destiny fails to take account of both the holy character of God and the fact that we are defiled in his sight.

Only when we see this do Jesus' words begin to make sense to us: 'No one comes to the Father....' The statement is universal. It includes not only those who heard him say it, but all of us. There are no exceptions. 'No one' is not merely a major limitation – only some can, or only a tiny minority can. *No one* means *not even one*.

But even Jesus qualifies this universal negative: 'except through me' (John 14:6). Surely Jesus is speaking here about 'coming to the Father' – what does that have to do with going to heaven? That question reveals a great deal about our spiritual condition.

Some time ago we heard a fascinating radio program in which a number of famous people were asked what they thought heaven would be like. A consistent three-point pattern began to emerge in their answers, although its most significant element seemed to pass unnoticed by the program makers:

1. All those interviewed believed in heaven.
2. All those interviewed assumed they would be there.
3. When asked to describe heaven, not one of those interviewed mentioned that God was there.

But it is the presence of God in holy, loving majesty that makes heaven what it is. It can even be said that

40

heaven is the presence of God – being in heaven means living with him for ever.

The Only Savior

Jesus Christ said that he is the One through whom we must come in order to be with the Father. This is the essential condition for our going to heaven. Those who hope that they can enter heaven in some other way than through his grace will be sorely disappointed (Matt. 7:21-23). If we are genuinely concerned to be there, we will take him at his word and come to the Father through him.

Jesus also explains why he alone can bring us to heaven. He is the way, the truth, and the life (John 14:6); he is the way to the Father, the truth of the Father, and life itself in the Father – for eternity!

Christ is the way. He alone is able to bridge the infinite gap between our sin and the Father's holiness. As the infinite and eternal Son of God, he came from the glory that he enjoyed with the Father to be made in the likeness of sinful man (Rom. 8:3). In his death on the cross, he paid the penalty that sin deserves.

Christ's obedience, credited to us, builds a bridge to the bliss of heavenly life with him. He paved the way in his self-denying act of leaving heaven and emptying himself by taking our nature. He humbled himself in obedience to his Father, even to the point of being willing to die a penal death on the cross under the terrible weight of guilt (Phil. 2:6-8). This led to his resurrection and ascension through which he entered heaven and opened it up to us. Thus, Jesus Christ is the only way for sinful men and women to come back to the Father. He offered himself as an acceptable sacrifice for our sins to his Father. He now lives in the Father's presence, interceding for his people (Rom. 8:34; Heb. 7:25).

Christ is the truth. He alone is able to show us the true state of our condition before God. His sinless life shows us the true nature of a world that is gripped by sin and is under the dominion of the powers of darkness and death.

Our sinfulness blinds us and deceives us into thinking that we are acceptable to God. Only Christ, who on the cross became unacceptable for us, can reveal to us our lost and unacceptable condition. Of course, we learn about sin and its consequences from God's law. But its full meaning hits us only when we see what the cross involved. There 'God made him who had no sin to be sin for us' (2 Cor. 5:21). There Christ came under the divine curse (Gal. 3:13). His death *for sin* shows us the truth about our condition *in sin*. But that same death *for* sin can save us *from* sin so that we become acceptable to the Father and fit for heaven.

Christ is the life. He alone provides the link between here and now and there and then. Often when Jesus speaks about 'life' he means a quality of existence altogether different from our present experience. In biblical usage, 'life' means closeness to the Life-giver and not just mere existence. When Scripture speaks of 'eternal life' it is speaking of the never-ending experience of intimate fellowship with God and his people. Apart from this, Paul tells us, we are dead to God even though we 'live' (cf. Eph. 2:1-4). From the

42

biblical point of view, even those who die without Christ still live, though their life is simply a shell that momentarily covers eternal death in outer darkness!

No wonder then that Christ refers to himself as *the* life, since only through him can we enjoy and maintain intimacy with the Father and be assured of an eternity with him. Our own confidence in our right to heaven is no guarantee that we will arrive there. He alone can provide the way to the Father in heaven.

Our Work or Christ's Work?

By contrast with Jesus' teaching, some religions tell us that the way to heaven is by our own efforts. Such efforts may take the form of personal discipline and sacrifice, humanitarian acts, sincerity or honesty in one's beliefs, or even gifts to charity. But according to Jesus, there is nothing we can contribute to our salvation. No matter what we offer to God it will never be adequate enough to compensate for our sins. Anything that we do is tainted and inadequate. It will always be unacceptable to the God who is too holy to look upon evil.

The sacrifice of Christ was acceptable to God. When he came, his life was one of complete obedience to God's will, worthy of acceptance by his Father. He lived a perfect life. He always loved the Lord his God with all his heart, soul, mind, and strength. He perfectly kept the commandments. He worshiped God alone. He never took his name in vain. He never worshiped a graven image. He always kept the Sabbath holy. He always honored his father and his mother. He never murdered. He never committed adultery. He never stole. He never lied. He never coveted (Exod. 20:1-17). He was perfect in every way, at every moment of his life on earth.

Adam was created to live like that. God placed him in an environment that made such obedience easy. Everything was in his favor. But he sinned and fell.

The Gospels vividly portray how Jesus' obedience was forged in the very different context of a fallen world. He too was tempted by Satan – but in an inhospitable environment: he was in the wilderness, not a garden; he was hungry, not surrounded by fruit; wild beasts roved over the terrain, not the animals who had come docilely to be named by Adam. Yet Jesus did not succumb to even the fiercest temptation, either in heart or in action.

No one has been or can ever be as obedient to the God of heaven as was Jesus. But he was not only obedient, 'he was obedient to death.' He chose to die rather than disobey. More than that, he was obedient to death, 'even death on a cross' (Phil. 2:8). God could, in perfect holiness, have chosen to condemn us all. But because of his great grace, he determined that the sacrifice of his Son would be sufficient payment for the sins committed by his people. So, the mission of the Son of God was to give his life a ransom for many (Mark 10:45).

Jesus did not need to die for his own sins. Since he remained sinless, he could therefore bear the burden of the guilt of our sinfulness on his back. This he willingly did, even though in the Garden of Gethsemane every natural human instinct in him shrank from the suffering involved (Mark 14:32-42). As a result, Christ was forsaken by his Father as he hung on the cross. His sense of abandonment was overwhelming. He cried out from the inner darkness of his experience into the outer darkness that symbolized God's covenant judgment against sin, 'My God, I am forsaken! Why?' (Matt. 27:46, authors' paraphrase).

The famous 'Suffering Servant' passage in Isaiah looks ahead to this sacrifice. The Servant was

> despised and rejected by men,
> a man of sorrows, and familiar with suffering.
> Like one from whom men hide their faces
> he was despised, and we esteemed him not
> (Isa. 53:3).

The reason for this soon becomes clear:

> But he was pierced for our transgressions,
> he was crushed for our iniquities;
> the punishment that brought us peace was upon him,
> and by his wounds we are healed (Isa. 53:5).

Why this litany of rejection and agony? The answer is, perhaps, the most surprising aspect of the Servant's suffering:

> [I]t was the LORD's will to crush him and cause him
> to suffer (Isa. 53:10).

There can be no mistake that Christ's death on the cross was the will of his Father. The Messiah suffered because the Lord willed it so. The cross of Christ was no accident.

But why would the Lord will such a thing for his dear Son? Because in eternity God set his unfailing love on sinners and determined that he would save them from the eternal loss for which they were otherwise destined. Only the love of God can explain the cross. It is because God loved the world that he gave his Son. And this love guarantees that those who come to Christ will spend eternity with him. 'In love,' says the apostle, 'he predestined us to be adopted as his sons through Jesus Christ, in accordance with his pleasure and will' (Eph. 1:4-5). Not only did the will of the Lord motivate the cross of Christ, but the will and pleasure of the Lord motivates our adoption into the family of his Son!

Living Faith

But what Christ has done does not bring us to heaven automatically or mechanically. How, then, do we come to share in the salvation that Jesus accomplished?

When Jesus died, two criminals were crucified beside him. Here is Luke's record of what happened:

One of the criminals who hung there hurled insults at him: 'Aren't you the Christ? Save yourself and us!' But the other criminal rebuked him. 'Don't you fear God,' he said, 'since you are under the same sentence? We are punished justly, for we are getting what our deeds deserve. But this man has done nothing wrong.' Then he said, 'Jesus, remember me when you come into your kingdom.' Jesus answered him, 'I tell you the truth, today you will be with me in paradise' (Luke 23:39-43).

46

In bitter anger one of the criminals was cursing Christ, but the other one began, lovingly, to defend Jesus. Amazingly, he realized that Jesus' death was different. He and his fellow criminal deserved to die, but Jesus had done nothing wrong. He was paying for transgressions he had never committed. More than that, the criminal saw that, despite the present humiliation, Jesus was a king. Thus, conscious of his own sin ('we are punished justly') he confessed and with trembling faith made his daring request: 'Jesus, remember me when you come into your kingdom.'

It was as if he had said, 'Lord, save me. Lord, take me with you to heaven,' for Jesus responded: 'today you will be with me in paradise.'

How grateful we ought to be that so-called death-bed conversions like this man's are still possible. Most Christian ministers, however, discover that they are quite rare. Most of us die as we have lived. It is quite unlikely that the Gospel writers record this story to encourage us to think we can postpone the issue of our own salvation until the last minute.

On the surface, the story of the dying thief's faith may not seem to be a typical example of how we can get to heaven. Yet in many ways this man's experience is a perfect illustration. He saw that he had sinned and deserved punishment. He saw that Christ was not suffering for the sins of others. Jesus was dying as an innocent man for the guilt of many. And, as the criminal's request shows, he knew that Christ was the King.

It was customary to nail to a criminal's cross the crime for which he was being executed. The notice on

Jesus' cross read: THIS IS JESUS, THE KING OF THE JEWS (Matt. 27:37). It was meant as mockery. One crucified criminal, however, realized that it was true, and so he asked to be remembered when Christ came into his kingdom. That was the request of a repentant man, a man who, by grace, recognized the Lord and realizing his own helplessness prayed, 'Jesus, remember me.' He even expressed his repentance in a practical way by defending Jesus as though he wanted to do whatever he could to comfort and encourage him in his death.

Jesus gave him a remarkable promise: 'today you will be with me in paradise.' That was even more than he had asked for. The man's request was for something in the future. Yet Christ's answer related directly to the present moment, '*today* you will be with me....' What a remarkable statement! Although his faith was new and in many ways still elementary, he was assured of a place with Christ in paradise on the very day of his request.

Eternal life with Christ came to the dying thief the moment he asked, in repentance and faith, to be remembered. For him, new life began the day he died. In that he was unusual. But what was true for him can be true for us: through faith in Christ crucified in our place, for our sins, we may receive forgiveness, new life, and the assurance of heaven. Today.

You Can Be Sure

Perhaps you know this because you have already come to living faith in Christ. Yet your assurance of heaven may be very weak; sometimes you are plagued with uncertainty. Can you really be sure that Christ will bring you into paradise? Yes, you can. Everything that Christ has done for us can be summed up in one word: grace. Grace is the holy Lord's looking down on people who are unholy and committing himself to them permanently. The death of Christ for us proves the intensity of his commitment (Rom. 8:32). If he has gone to these lengths for us, we can be sure he will never let us go.

Why, then, do some Christians lack assurance of heaven? Sometimes the answer lies in the way we think about our salvation. We came to Christ '... by grace, through faith' (Eph. 2:8). But now we look at our lives, at our behavior patterns, and conclude that we are still unacceptable to God. We begin to doubt if heaven really awaits us.

By thinking like this we are turning the gospel on its head. It is by grace we have been saved, not by our own holiness. Our assurance of heaven does not depend on our achievements, even our Christian achievements – it depends on Christ. Of course, a changed life provides evidence that we really are saved, but it can never be a completely secure anchor for our assurance because our holiness is always fragmentary. We must not allow our eyes to drift to what the Holy Spirit is doing in us to such an extent that we completely lose sight of the fundamental thing – what Christ has done for us.

So assurance of heaven will not come to us because we are better now than we were then (although with God's help we will be, whether we ourselves always see that or not). It will come to us because Christ died for us and assures us he will never turn away those who trust in him. No one will snatch us out of the Father's hand. He gives us that assurance (John 10:27-30). Do not look for it elsewhere!

Heaven can indeed be a sure thing. We can be sure of it only through Jesus Christ – it is promised only to those who put themselves, by faith, into his hands. Once we trust him, we are his and he is ours – for eternity!

But what will heaven be like? That is the next important question we must answer.

4

WHAT WILL HEAVEN BE LIKE?

> Now I lay me down to sleep,
> I pray the Lord my soul to keep;
> If I should die before I wake,
> I pray the Lord my soul to take.

Children have been taught to say these words for over 200 years now. It may well be the only prayer some people know. It is a prayer for mercy and for grace at the time of death. It is also a prayer that suggests there is a mystery involved in death. Tonight I may lay my head down on the pillow at the end of a day's work – perhaps full of joy and success, or of frustration and discouragement – and during the night my earthly life may end: the Lord may take my soul to heaven.

What will heaven be like? Almost every parent is asked that question, and they certainly ought to think about it a great deal. We would be ashamed if we short-changed our children with poor answers to other important questions. If they ask us about what they should do with their lives, what profession to pursue, or whether they should marry, we would do all in our power to help and guide them. The same should be true in regard to heaven.

We must, however, frame the question more precisely if we are to answer it accurately. Left to ourselves we can know nothing about heaven. How could we, without divine revelation? But divine revelation is exactly what has been given to us in Scripture. When we ask what the *Bible* says heaven will be like, we may be surprised at how much it has to say.

Perhaps we should begin with the obvious.

God with Us

One of the most basic things the Bible teaches is that God is present with his people. This is so obvious that we often take it for granted or overlook it altogether. But when it dawns on us how holy God is and how sinful we are, we begin to marvel at the fact that God is *with* us.

Moses discovered this in a profound way. After he had been commissioned to lead God's people, the Lord commanded him: 'Leave this place, you and the people you brought up out of Egypt, and go up to the land I promised on oath to Abraham, Isaac and Jacob, saying, "I will give it to your descendants"' (Exod. 33:1). Moses had grave reservations about whether he could accomplish such a task and replied, 'You have been telling me, 'Lead these people,' but you have not let me know whom you will send with me' (Exod. 33:12). He needed someone to be with him, to support him, to be his guide, and even to be his spokesman as he sought to accomplish the Lord's will.

But Moses realized that he had an even deeper need for the presence of the Lord: 'If your Presence does not go with us, do not send us up from here' (Exod. 33:15). In effect he was saying, 'Lord, if you don't go with me, I don't want to go.' Notice his reasoning: 'How will anyone know that you are pleased with me and with your people unless you go with us? What else will distinguish me and your people from all the other people on the face of the earth?' (Exod. 33:16).

He understood the significance of God's presence. It is what makes his people different. Apart from God's presence there was no reason for obedience. King David later shared that conviction: his only security when he walked through the darkest valley was the assurance 'you are with me' (Ps. 23:4).

In the New Testament, too, the presence of God is the central characteristic of Christ's church. His people are identified by the indwelling of the Holy Spirit. Christ comes to be with us and to indwell us through his Spirit, making us his temple, bringing us into his family, creating a unique international fellowship of people set apart for his service. In one sense everything Christ accomplished for us was with a view to his coming to dwell in us. That is why the theme of his indwelling his people is so prominent in the teaching he gave in the upper room shortly before his death. He promised that through the gift of his Spirit at Pentecost he would be present with his people. God redeems his people in order to dwell among them.

Moses understood this. That is why he pled for the presence of God. But immediately after the Lord promised that he would be with him, Moses said, quite spontaneously, 'Now show me your glory' (Exod. 33:18). The promise of God's special presence produced a longing to see the glory of God. Why? Because God's glory is the full manifestation of all that his presence means. To see God's glory is simply to experience his presence more fully.

Every believer who experiences the presence of God develops an appetite to taste it again more fully. That is what a desire for the glory of God is. It is why Jesus prayed that his disciples would not only experience his indwelling presence, 'I in them and you in me' (John 17:23), but also that they would experience his glory, 'Father, I want those you have given me to be with me ... and to see my glory' (John 17:24).

Do you see how this illumines our understanding of what heaven will be like? God is present with his people now. The Spirit of the Father and the Son indwells his people in a special way (John 14:23). His presence produces in us a longing to see his glory. Heaven is the ultimate answer to that longing because being in his presence and seeing his glory will be one and the same thing.

In one sense, of course, God's presence is unlimited. He is omnipresent, or everywhere present. David speaks about this at length in Psalm 139: there is no 'where' in the universe from which God is excluded. But the omnipresence of God is not the same as his presence with his people. God is with them in a very special way. He is with them, according to his covenant promise, to bless them!

Divine Blessing

One of the earliest and most quoted benedictions or 'blessing formulas' in Scripture is the Aaronic benediction, which the High Priest was given to pronounce in God's name. It is a rich and beautiful blessing. Each successive statement in it says the same thing in a different and more heightened way than the previous one:

> The LORD bless you
>   and keep you;
> the LORD make his face shine upon
>   you and be gracious to you;
> the LORD turn his face towards you
>   and give you peace (Num. 6:24-26).

'The LORD bless you and keep you' conveys the most basic truth about the presence of God: he is good to his people and he cares deeply for them. Each of the following lines thereafter says this again, in a somewhat different and richer way, explaining what it means to be blessed and kept by God's presence.

'The LORD make his face shine upon you and be gracious to you....' Here the blessing and keeping of the Father is expressed on his face, which shines with grace and joy as he extends his blessing to us. He is glad, not reluctant, to love his people. Most children know that some parental looks speak far more, and at times hurt far more, than any other action could. The principle here is the same. The look or the shine of the Father's face is expressed in the way he both accepts us as his children and governs our lives. To know that the heavenly Father smiles on us with pleasure is surely the richest experience that a Christian could ever have. To know that the Father so delights in us that he wants to come by his Spirit to be at home in our lives (John 14:23) far exceeds all earthly pleasures combined. To be blessed and kept is to experience the pleasure of God as a loving, caring, smiling Father. His face shines on us, his love surrounds us, and he is gracious to us.

The last line of Aaron's blessing formula further expands on the first: 'The LORD turn his face towards you and give you peace.' Even more painful than a parent's look of disappointment is no look at all. The same is true of the heavenly Father. The thought that he might never look at us is more than we can bear. Thankfully, however, the face of God has been lifted up toward us. Although he could turn his back on us because of our sin, he does not. Instead he turned his back on his own Son, who bore our guilt and judgment on the cross.

Think what this means: when Jesus went into the presence of God as our sin-bearer the Aaronic blessing was reversed:

| The Lord *bless* you and *keep* you; The Lord make his face *shine* upon you and *be gracious* to you; The Lord turn his face *towards* you and give you *peace*. | Became | The Lord *curse* you and *forsake* you; The Lord make his face *frown* upon you and *condemn* you; The Lord turn his face *away from* you and give you *grief*. |

Now we experience the blessing of his countenance that looks graciously on us. Not only does his face shine, but it shines towards us. Not only is his countenance lifted up, but it is lifted up toward us. With a loving glance, he gives us peace. This is not a temporary peace. It is the final peace by which we are reconciled to the God who was formerly our enemy.

When we think through the implications of this, we begin to see the reason why heaven is so glorious:

> [S]ince we have been justified through faith, we have peace with God through our Lord Jesus Christ, through whom we have gained *access* by faith into this grace in which we now stand. And we rejoice in the hope of the glory of God.
>
> (Rom. 5:1-2, emphasis added)

As for Moses, so for us, the blessing of God's presence is the blessing of his face that gazes on us and lovingly approves us in Christ. This brings peace. No wonder, then, that Moses cried for the Lord's presence to be with him. No wonder, then, that the promise of God's presence led Moses to ask to see God's glory. What would he not give for just a sight of his face?

God's Family

But this is a book about heaven. What does all this have to do with heaven? It has everything to do with it because the biblical teaching on life after death is less concerned about where we will be than it is about whose we will be.

Christians are God's children. He is our Father and gives us the Spirit of adoption (Rom. 8:15-17; Gal. 4:4-7). The Holy Spirit now indwells us and is the guarantee that we will dwell with God for eternity (Eph. 1:13-14).

Think of this in terms of Jesus' famous words in John 14:1-3. This is a favorite passage of Scripture for many people because of the comfort and peace about which it speaks:

> Let not your heart be troubled: ye believe in God, believe also in me. In my Father's house are many mansions: if it were not so, I would have told you. I go to prepare a place for you. And if I go and prepare a place for you, I will come again, and receive you unto myself; that where I am, there ye may be also (KJV).

What is this mansion in heaven that God has prepared for us? The Greek word translated *mansion* in John 14:2 occurs only in this chapter of the New Testament. The fundamental idea is not so much that we have a *house* (a mansion) in heaven but that our *home* is there.

We all instinctively know the difference between a house and a home, even if we find it difficult to define. When people ask us where our home is we usually tell them where our family is. That is what makes a place home for us. It is not merely a house. What Jesus promises his disciples is not merely a house in heaven. He is emphasizing the nature of the relationship that we enjoy there – it will be home.

The only other occurrence of the word translated *mansion* is in John 14:23:

> Jesus answered and said unto him, 'If a man love me, he will keep my words: and my Father will love him, and we will come unto him, and make our abode with him' (KJV).

Abode means *home*. What Christ refers to is the deepening of our relationship with him and his Father that takes place when we love him and keep his commandments.

Jesus is really speaking about the same thing earlier in the chapter. He tells his troubled disciples that he is going away, not to build a house, but to prepare for the deepening of the relationship they will experience once his work in them here is finished. He is telling them that heaven will be a richer and fuller relationship with God than anything they will ever experience here on earth!

Part of the answer to the question, 'What will heaven be like?' is, therefore, that it will be the enjoyment of this perfect relationship. It will be a situation in which you will never be lonely, never lack company, never feel isolated, and always be completely content in God's presence. All of the relationships enjoyed in heaven, between Christ, others, and you, will be perfect in every way!

When we learn to see that the essence of being in heaven is the flowering and consummation of our relationship with the Lord, we begin to appreciate the riches that will be ours when we are there. This, incidentally, has the opposite effect on our lives from the one most people expect. There is a clever saying that people are so heavenly minded they are no earthly use. That is quite false. Scripture gives us a completely different perspective: our real problem is that we are not sufficiently heavenly minded. The discovery of all that awaits us in heaven makes a radical difference in the way we live here and now. We begin to focus our attention on the things that are truly and lastingly important. Life after death is, in this way, intimately connected to life before death. Focusing on heaven as a relationship allows us to see other things more clearly.

The Soul

Ask a Christian the question, 'What happens to your soul when you die?' This is obviously a 'set-up,' and most of us are a little hesitant to answer. What trap is being set for us in these words? If someone attempts an answer, it is usually something like this: 'It goes to heaven,' or 'It goes to be with Christ,' or some similar words. In a sense this is true, but it reveals a way of thinking that the question is actually designed to highlight.

Ask the question again, this time in a different way: 'If when you die, your soul goes to heaven, where are you?' 'In heaven,' is the usual response. Of course! But the earlier answer said that 'it' goes to heaven. Do we change from being a person to being an 'it' when we die? The point, of course, is that when we die, we ourselves – not some impersonal part of us – go to be with Christ.

Consider Paul's words when he was thinking about the possibility of his own death. He knew that to live was Christ. He also knew that to die was gain. His central emphasis is on his personal relationship with Christ.

> Yet what shall I choose? I do not know! I am torn between the two: I desire to depart and be with Christ, which is better by far; but it is more necessary for you that I remain in the body (Phil. 1:22-24).

Paul longs to depart and be with Christ, but it is necessary that *he* remain in the body. There is no hint here of some *thing* going to heaven but rather of Paul himself going to be with his Lord. The 'gain' of which he speaks is the presence of Christ, deeper and richer in heaven than anything he has experienced here on earth. When Christians die, therefore, we go to be with Christ. But we are not yet all that we will be. We are with Christ, but the final harvest remains to be gathered.

We have now learned three crucial things about our lives after death:

1. Our relationship with Christ is richer and deeper because of our entrance into his presence.
2. When we die as Christians, we (and not a 'part' of us) go to be with Christ.
3. Our life in heaven is not the end of the road for us. There is more to come.

Descriptions of Heaven

We have already begun to see that a major part of the answer to the question, 'What will heaven be like?' is that in heaven Christians will experience a deepened relationship with Christ. An old Lutheran scholar, J. A. Bengel, expressed this beautifully, commenting on Paul's words, 'To me to live is Christ and to die is gain,' when he wrote, 'To live is Christ; to die will be more Christ.' Thus, if someone asks what heaven will be like, it is appropriate to ask what life with Christ is like for us now.

Does that question confuse you? If it does, you must try to grasp the heart of the issue. You want to go to heaven. But heaven is dominated by Christ and his presence. It is for those who love him and for whom his presence is everything. It is living forever with Christ in loving fellowship and worship. How can you believe that you will want heaven *then* if you do not want Christ *now*?

But what if Christ does mean everything to us? Then heaven will be the amplification and consummation of our relationship with him. We experience his presence and grace now; we will enjoy them to the full then. Think of occasions when you have been especially conscious of the grace and love of God. The experience of heaven is the extending, fulfilling, and perpetuating of that.

Christian biographies bear eloquent witness to this fact. Each Christian finds his or her own way to express it. The North African, Augustine, spoke of his heart's finding rest; the German, Martin Luther, spoke of the gates of paradise opening; the Frenchman, Blaise Pascal, spoke of fire; the Englishman, John Wesley, felt his heart 'strangely warmed.' Isaac Watts taught the church to sing about it: 'The men of grace have found glory begun below.' Heaven is the consummation of these experiences of Christ; its joys come from seeing him face to face.

When people ask the question, 'What is heaven like?' they usually expect an answer that has more to do with heaven's physical characteristics, rather than the fulfilled relationship with Christ that dominates it. We need to remember that heaven means that we will be at home with God. Heaven is not merely a house.

The Vision of Revelation

The book of Revelation contains various descriptions of what heaven is like. Chapters four, five, and six present us with a particularly vivid portrayal of its glory.

In this wonderful vision, John sees heaven through an open door. He enters the divine presence. Before him stands a magnificent throne. Someone glorious is sitting on it. Peals of thunder crash around it; flashes of lightning come from it. Four mysterious living creatures surround it, and seem to act as worship leaders:

Day and night they never stop saying:

'Holy, holy, holy
is the Lord God Almighty,
who was, and is, and is to come.'

Whenever the living creatures give glory, honor, and thanks to him who sits on the throne and who lives for ever and ever, the twenty-four elders fall down before him who sits on the throne, and worship him who lives for ever and ever. They lay their crowns before the throne and say:

> 'You are worthy, our Lord and God,
> to receive glory and honor and power,
> for you created all things,
> and by your will they were created
> and have their being' (Rev. 4:8-11).

This is rich, picturesque language, full of symbols. But its purpose is obvious: to communicate to us the worship and praise that those in heaven instinctively give, all day, every day (and even all night) to the One who sits on the throne. It is immediately clear that heaven is a place of continual worship.

Something happens in chapter 6 that adds to the drama. Jesus Christ, described as the Lamb who was slain, begins to open the seven seals that secure the book of God's providence. When he opens the fifth seal, we are given further indications of what happens in heaven.

> When he opened the fifth seal, I saw under the altar the souls of those who had been slain because of the word of God and the testimony they had maintained. They called out in a loud voice, 'How long, Sovereign Lord, holy and true, until you judge the inhabitants of the earth and avenge our blood?' Then each of them was given a white robe, and they were told to wait a little longer, until the number of their fellow servants and brothers who were to be killed as they had been was completed (Rev. 6:9-11).

There are many aspects of the book of Revelation that seem very mysterious, but several things in this passage are clear.

When the Lamb opens the fifth seal, we see a group in heaven. This is no longer the same scene as the one described in chapter 5. There people were exclusively occupied with giving praise and worship to God the Creator. Here they are crying out to the Lord. They do not seem to be engaged directly in worship. Instead they 'called out in a loud voice, 'How long ... until you judge?''

These souls in heaven are not portrayed as *complaining*, but rather as *praying*. They address the Sovereign Lord in the same way we do when we cry out to him in prayer as his children. In fact, the verb used here for the calling out of the saints is the same one Paul uses when he speaks about God's children crying, '*Abba*, Father' (Rom. 8:15). In our crying out we simply mirror our Savior who, with loud crying and tears, lifted up his voice to heaven, saying, '*Abba*, Father' (Mark 14:36; Heb. 5:7).

The Coming Kingdom

Here and now we live in between Christ's first coming and the unknown time of his second coming. The book of Revelation suggests that in some mysterious way that tension continues until the final consummation of all things. This is confirmed even from the viewpoint of those who are already in heaven. Indeed, tension will continue until Christ is again revealed at the end of the age and creates the new heavens and the new earth.

We must not make the mistake of thinking that saints are complaining and murmuring in heaven. Consider their question, 'How long, Sovereign Lord, holy and true, until you judge the inhabitants of the earth and avenge our blood?' (Rev. 6:10) in the context of the Lord's Prayer. We pray: 'Thy kingdom come, Thy will be done on earth as *it is* in heaven' (Matt. 6:10 KJV). In these words, we ask that the Father will bring his kingdom to its fullest expression *on the earth*. That petition will be answered only on the day when Christ 'hands over the kingdom to God the Father after he has destroyed all dominion, authority and power' (1 Cor. 15:24).

These petitions, therefore, are not prayers of complaining or murmuring; nor are they primarily calls for vengeance. The martyrs under the altar are not complaining because the Lord has not given them their due. They are longing for the coming of his kingdom, or better, the coming of the King himself, our Lord Jesus Christ, and for the consummation of God's purposes throughout history. These petitions are requests for the glory of God to find its perfect manifestation on earth. They are based on the sure promises of God and on the fact that Christ has promised that he will come again.

That is what these martyred souls in heaven are praying for. They are asking for the fulfillment of the kingdom of God. Then God's justice will be fully displayed. Their primary concern for the coming of Christ's kingdom is his glory, not their personal relief. And so it will be in heaven for us as we await our final destiny.

Here, then, is part of the Bible's own answer to the question, 'What will heaven be like?' There we will worship the Lord free from the sloth and coldness we experience now. We will enjoy living in his presence without the weakness, shame, and guilt of sin we now know. Ours will be the privilege of serving and adoring the One who made us and who redeemed us in love.

There is, however, another aspect to life in heaven. While we will honor and adore God, we will also be conscious that we have not yet arrived at the place of our final destiny. And so, like those under the altar, we will pray that the Lord will soon bring about the end of this world and the beginning of the world to come. We will pray that his reign will be fully realized over his entire creation. We will ask, 'How long, Lord?'

Like many people today, we sometimes have to spend extended periods away from our families. The time seems to drag slowly, even though there are telephone calls, letters, cards, and even electronic mail along the way. Communication may indeed be frequent, but it is not the same as being with the family. On one such occasion, one of us returned to his family, but for a variety of reasons was not able to go back to his house immediately. But the sight of a much-loved and missed wife waiting at the airport was enough. It was insignificant that the *house* could not be occupied. As long as *she* and *the family* were there, it was home!

Heaven will be like that. The satisfying of our curiosity about the physical circumstances is far less significant than the fact that Christ himself will be there, with his family. He will welcome us with open arms to our home. Our communication will no longer be faceless and through the printed word. We will see Christ as he is, face to face. Our greatest joy will be to express our love for him and to worship and serve him in the presence of his entire family.

'What is heaven like?' It is like going home – to Christ!

There is more to come, as we shall see. In fact there is so much more that words from James Barrie's famous play *Peter Pan* will be wonderfully true for Christians: 'To die will be an awfully big adventure.'

5

THE BEST IS YET TO BE

One of our friends overheard a conversation between an affluent upper-middle-class lady and a young boy from a housing project. He was staring at a group of luxury houses, one of which belonged to the lady. Pointing to them, he asked, 'Do you live in that housing project?' She was horrified! How could anyone describe the beautiful residence on which she had lavished so much expense and care as part of a housing project?

It is just as hard for us in our western this-worldly horizoned society to believe that, by comparison with what God will do in the future, this world is but a housing project, vandalized by man. However magnificent, real, and lasting it may seem from our present perspective, it is a shadow of the reality that is yet to be.

Can we take this in? We tend to see things through the wrong end of the telescope. For us it is what we see and feel just now that seems real, solid, and permanent. The world to come seems unreal, insubstantial, and almost a daydream by comparison. When we look through biblical lenses, however, we discover how myopic we have been. There we learn that our present experiences are 'not worth comparing with the glory that will be revealed in us' (Rom. 8:18). By comparison with the weight of that glory, our present sufferings are light and momentary. It is the as-yet-invisible, not the already-visible that is eternal (2 Cor. 4:17-18).

Our problem is that our sense of values has been distorted. We treasure the visible and ephemeral; we discount the invisible and eternal. That is why we need to listen again to the injunction not to be conformed to this age, but to be transformed through the renewing of our minds (Rom. 12:1-2). The biblical doctrine of the final state is intended to reverse our this-age mentality.

In the New Testament, the key to understanding what God will do in the future lies in the resurrection of Jesus, which is described as 'the first-foots' of a harvest that is still to come. Jesus is the prototype of something that will take place on a vast scale.

Think of the now-famous words of Neil Armstrong, the first man to set foot on the moon. He was a trailblazer and spoke of his achievement as 'one small step for man, one giant leap for mankind.' The significance of man's setting foot on the moon pales into insignificance when compared to Christ's first step outside the garden tomb. His resurrection on Easter day is not only the cause of our spiritual resurrection today (1 Pet. 1:3) but is also the first-fruits of a resurrection harvest on the last day. In the resurrection of Jesus, the powers of darkness were dramatically and suddenly thrown into reverse. The Divine Future broke into the present, and an event that belonged to the end of the ages – resurrection – arrived early in Christ.

Christ, the First Resurrection

The central significance of Jesus' resurrection lies in the fact that it is just the beginning of the saving, renewing, resurrecting work of God that will have its climax in the restoration of the entire cosmos.

Paul discusses this in a remarkable passage:

> Christ has indeed been raised from the dead, the first-fruits of those who have fallen asleep. For since death came through a man, the resurrection of the dead comes also through a man. For as in Adam all die, so in Christ all will be made alive. But each in his own turn: Christ, the first-fruits; then, when he comes, those who belong to him. Then the end will come, when he hands over the kingdom to God the Father after he has destroyed all dominion, authority and power. For he must reign until he has put all his enemies under his feet. The last enemy to be destroyed is death. For he 'has put everything under his feet.' Now when it says that 'everything' has been put under him, it is clear that this does not include God himself, who put everything under Christ. When he has done this, then the Son himself will be made subject to him who put everything under him, so that God may be all in all (1 Cor. 15:20-28).

Here the apostle is explaining that what will happen in the future will involve the rescuing and restoration of what was lost in the past. The divine order will be both re-established and consummated. Notice the five stages in which this will take place:

First, the resurrection of Christ begins the reversal of the death that was introduced into the world by Adam (vv. 22-23).

Second, that grand reversal will bring about the destruction of all of Christ's enemies, 'all dominion, authority and power,' including death (vv. 24-26).

Third, having subdued everything that stood against God, Christ will offer a subjugated world to his Father (v. 24).

Fourth, the Son will then himself become subject to the Father (v. 28). This is one of the most staggering statements in the entire New Testament: the Son will be subject to the Father! But this does not mean that the Son of God in his divine nature is inferior – a kind of secondary deity – to the Father. The picture is more subtle and more beautiful.

Before creation, the triune God was all in all for himself and to himself, living in a perfect fellowship, deeply content within his divine being. But then creation, with human beings – God's image – as its apex, was the Father's love gift to his Son (Col. 1:16; Heb. 1:2-3). In turn, man was given the privileged role of being the steward of the Son's world; he had dominion over it (Gen. 1:28). But, through humanity's disobedience, the cosmos became a rebel creation, gone astray from the Father's will and therefore from the Son's lordship.

The Father and Son, who live and love together in the fellowship of the Spirit, planned a work of restoration. The Son would take on human nature in order to serve as our substitute before God. He would obey in our place, and then accept the punishment for our disobedience – the death penalty, even the shameful death on the cross.

He would do what Adam failed to do; he would undo the consequences of what Adam had done. That is why Paul calls him the second man and the last Adam (1 Cor. 15:45, 47).

Once the full penalty for our sin had been paid in death, the Father would raise him up again and glorify him for his loving obedience. Now risen and exalted, the Son incarnate subdues everything to himself once more. By the power of his Spirit the ends of the earth become his inheritance (Ps. 2:8; Matt. 28:18-20). When this work is brought to its grand climax at Christ's return, he will not only offer his world back to the Father in triumph, but as the incarnate Son yield himself to his Father in love.

Fifth, God will then be manifested as all in all (1 Cor. 15:28). In the restoration, the triune God, who before creation lived in and to himself, will now be seen to be all in all to the renewed creation. This is also the thrust of the vision of the closing two chapters of the book of Revelation. There the old order passes away and God is seen to be Alpha and Omega, the Beginning and the End, the All in All.

This final cosmic order will be ushered in by the return of Christ. He will come personally, visibly, audibly, and gloriously. The dead will be raised (Dan. 12:2; John 5:25-29; Acts 24:15; Rev. 20:11-15) and living believers will be transformed (1 Cor. 15:51). All men will appear before the great white throne (Rev. 20:11), which is elsewhere described as the judgment seat of God (Rom. 14:10), and – in view of John 5:22

– is also identical with the judgment seat of Christ (2 Cor. 5:10). Then the decision will be announced in which all will discover what is due them for the deeds they have done while in the body. This will serve as a prelude to the actual reception of those things in the new heavens and new earth, or in the judgment of the lake of fire and the outer darkness (Rev. 21-22).

The two ways of life and death that run through Scripture will thus permanently divide. The righteous and the wicked, the sheep and the goats, the wheat and the tares, will be irrevocably distinguished. The blessed will stand on the right hand in the position of favor; others will be on the left in shame and dishonor. Scripture speaks clearly and forcefully about this division, but the clarity of its revelation is greatest in relation to what takes place at the right hand of God.

The Resurrection of Believers

When Christ returns, the resurrection of all who have died will take place; the dead in Christ will be raised and those in Christ who are still alive will be changed, 'in a flash' as Paul puts it (1 Cor. 15:52). All believers will be transformed, whether they are alive or dead.

Paul discusses this resurrection change in 1 Corinthians 15:35-49 in answer to the question, 'How are the dead raised and with what kind of body?' What is involved in the change?

He appeals first to patterns that God has established in nature: seeds die, flowers are their resurrection life. In addition, the natural order teaches us that not all bodily existence is of the same kind. All earthly bodies (flesh) are of the same genus, although there

THE BEST IS YET TO BE

are different species (v. 39). All heavenly bodies (sun, moon, and stars) are of the same genus, but of different species (vv. 40-41). But earthly and heavenly bodies are of a different genus (v. 40).

Paul's point is that though there will be important points of continuity between the present body and the resurrection body, the resurrection body will belong to a different order of existence than does the earthly body. He sums up this difference in two terms that are difficult to capture in English: the present body is natural (*psychikon*); the future body is spiritual (*pneumatikon*). This contrast is further enlarged in three ways:

Present Body	Future Body
Perishable	Imperishable
Dishonorable	Honorable
Weak	Powerful

The durability, honor, and strength of our present bodily existence is a temporary illusion. It is permeated by our present sinful weakness. It is a poor, unattractive seed and must give way to the imperishable, honorable, and powerful flower of the resurrected person.

These are not merely theoretical statements. As Paul points out, they are conclusions drawn from what took place in the prototype (1 Cor. 15:49). In Christ, God has already given us a life-size working model as it were, for what Paul says of the resurrection change is dependent on what he has learned from Christ's resurrection change. Just as we have borne the likeness of Adam, the man of dust, says Paul, we shall bear the

75

likeness of the man from heaven. Christ's resurrection is not only the first resurrection, it is the cause of which our resurrection is the inevitable effect. By the power of the Spirit, the risen Christ will transform our bodies to be like his glorious body (Phil. 3:21).

The Resurrection Body

What will this body be like? We are not the first to ask that question. Paul tells us it will be spiritual, glorious, unrecognizable.

Spiritual

Paul calls the resurrection body a spiritual body (in Greek, *soma pneumatikon – a pneumatic body*). We do not know what this means biologically and biochemically. Perhaps we should only guardedly draw implications from the narratives in Luke 24:36-43 and John 20:27 in which the resurrection body of Christ bears wounds, can be touched, and is capable of consuming food. These passages confirm the claim that Christ's resurrection was bodily, rather than emphasize the most important characteristics of the resurrection body. By calling it 'spiritual' Paul does not mean ethereal, ghostlike, or insubstantial. The word should probably have a capital *S – Spiritual*. It means *appropriate to the world of the Holy Spirit*. A spiritual body is one that is freed from the weakness of the flesh, and whose behavior reveals the lordship of the Holy Spirit. The essence of its pneumatic nature is that it is raised by the Spirit in power (Rom. 8:11; Phil. 3:21).

Just as Christ was declared Son of God with power by the Spirit of holiness in the resurrection (Rom. 1:4), so the redemption or resurrection of our bodies (Rom. 8:23) is God's declaration, and the final proof, that we are the sons that God has adopted with power. Just as Jesus was crucified in weakness but lives by God's power, so we who share in his weakness will also share in the power of the resurrection (Phil. 3:10-11), the power of an indestructible life (2 Cor. 13:4).

We have no measure by which we can assess what this means. Even those who were brought back to life by Jesus himself were restored only to a weak humanity. Lazarus continued to feel weary, was liable to disease, and later died. The final resurrection, however, is not merely a resuscitation – it is transformation. It releases us from the body of death and clothes us in a body of life.

We have a friend who went to his physician complaining of an ongoing sense of general physical lethargy. In the course of some tests, his doctors discovered that he was not breathing an adequate supply of oxygen when he was sleeping. He thus had to sleep wearing an appliance that enabled him to inhale an adequate supply of oxygen. At first he found this uncomfortable, but the transformation in him was remarkable. The lethargy disappeared. He had actually begun to feel that his lethargic state was normal. Now he comments: 'I can't believe how great truly normal life is!'

In some ways resurrection life will be like that transformation. The resurrection body will be full of power and energy. Living in the Spirit, so that our still-sinful and weakened bodies serve as his temple, is a struggle for us now. We have to battle against sin and Satan. Some of us struggle with depressing, long-term physical disabilities. We long to be set free. But then, in a body that is adapted completely to a life of holiness and fellowship with God through the Spirit, obedience will be natural. Indeed, it will be easy!

Glorious

The redemption of the body by its resurrection is part of what Paul calls the glorious liberty of the children of God (Rom. 8:18). Just as we now inherit the sufferings of Christ, we shall also inherit his glory (Rom. 8:23).

Paul traces this theme of glory very carefully through the first eight chapters of Romans. Man was made for the glory of God, but has exchanged it for idolatry (1:21-23). He has fallen short of God's glory (3:23). But in Christ the hope of sharing in glory has been restored (5:2); now this glory is certain (8:30). Paul also speaks of the way this glory will be revealed in God's children (8:18, 21), when they are finally conformed to Christ (8:29). This is the resurrection glory that will be accomplished in us by the Spirit, consummating the transformation that he has already begun (2 Cor. 3:18; Rom. 8:11).

There are two aspects to glory, both of them inherent in the biblical portrayal. The first is transfiguration. On the mountain of transfiguration, Peter saw Christ receiving glory from God (2 Pet. 1:17). John likewise gazed on his glory as the glory of the only Son of the Father (John 1:14). Seeing him as the Living One who had been dead (Rev. 1:17-18), he was overwhelmed by the splendor of the sight. The resurrection body will reflect Christ's awe-inspiring holy beauty of which these men caught just a glimpse.

The second aspect, found in the Old Testament word for glory, is that of weightiness and worthiness – of substantiality. The resurrection body is an element in an inheritance that can never perish, spoil, or fade (1 Pet. 1:4). It is, we might say, a quality article. It will, for example, be able to bear the immediate vision of Christ. It will be suited to the eternal realm just as our present bodies are suited to the temporal. It will be made to last.

This new quality of life may give us a clue to our Lord's enigmatic statement that we will not marry or be given in marriage in heaven, since we will be like the angels (Matt. 22:30). These words have perplexed some Christians. Why should this great gift disappear in the future age when it has been a central creation gift from God?

Marriage is seen in the Bible as God's universal divine gift for man's loneliness (Gen. 2:18). It was also instituted to help in fellowship with and service to God. But in the new heavens and the new earth, when the dwelling place of God is with man, the functions of marriage will no more be required. No temple will be needed, because God will himself be with us (Rev. 21:3, 22). No sun will be needed because the glory of God and the presence of the Lamb will give light. These various gifts of the first creation will no longer be required in the second creation. Now they are pointers to immediate fellowship with God; but then, such will be the intimacy of our fellowship with God that they will be obsolete.

If that is true, how indescribably glorious and satisfying that fellowship must be!

Recognizable

'Will we be able to recognize each other in the future?' is a frequently asked question. If we think of Christ as the prototype, the answer seems obvious. He was recognizably the same person as the one the disciples had known and followed. When the angels spoke of his coming again at the end of the age they even described him as 'this same Jesus' (Acts 1:11). Recognizability is assumed in what Paul says of the resurrection body in 1 Corinthians 15:42-43. So the Westminster Confession of Faith affirms that 'the dead will be raised with the self-same bodies, and none other, although with different qualities' (32.2).

The resurrection of the body implies that we will be identifiably the very same persons we are now, even though we will not be constituted of precisely the same physical substance. Of course, as we know, we are not constituted of precisely the same material substance throughout the whole course of our present lives. The fact that we cut our nails and our hair indicates that. Yet there is continuity; we still remain the same bodily person. This is what the New Testament teaches.

But the spiritual, or pneumatic, body is a different genus from the physical, or psychical, body, as Paul makes clear in 1 Corinthians 15:39-44. It has different qualities, even though the believer remains identifiably the same bodily person.

Sometimes the question, 'Will we recognize one another?' arises out of a misconception that the Bible teaches the immortality of the soul. How can we hope to recognize someone's disembodied soul? Of course, in an important sense, the Bible does teach the immortality of the soul. And, yes, in an important sense the soul will be recognizable; knowing someone involves more than being able to identify his or her body. But the focus of Scripture is on a bodily resurrection, and this implies that we will have clearly recognizable personal characteristics.

Jesus was recognizable after the resurrection. True, neither Mary nor the two disciples en route to Emmaus recognized him, but in both cases this failure is regarded as unusual; it is due to specific reasons. When she heard Jesus' well-loved voice, Mary recognized him. When the disciples saw his hands as he broke the bread, they recognized him (John 20:10-18; Luke 24:19-35). Like Christ, we too will be recognizable after the resurrection. Indeed, who and what we really are will be clearer than ever.

Our present experience is creating for us an eternal weight of glory, says Paul (2 Cor. 4:17). The trials of this life are, as it were, the potter's hands molding us into something greater for the future. All that each of us has truly (but often invisibly) been, will be made clear in our personal share of resurrection glory.

Sometimes, in the course of our work, complete strangers will come to meet us at an airport. They may know us only from photographs they have seen. Quite often they will say, 'Why, you're much younger (or taller) than I expected.' When we meet one another in the final resurrection state, perhaps it will be a little like that. We will say with far greater depth of meaning: 'You seem to be much livelier and healthier than I remembered' because the Spirit will have made clear all his previously hidden work in our lives.

81

New Heavens, New Earth

Man was made from the dust of the earth; like the animal creation, we are living souls, or beings. Yet we are also the image of God. Inextricably part of creation, we also transcend it. We were made to be creation's link to God, to rule creation on God's behalf, and to express intelligently creation's praise and obedience. When humanity fell and shattered God's kind covenant with us, we brought down the whole of creation with us; the curse fell on the very dust from which we emerged as well as on ourselves. Subjection, bondage, and decay were all elements in Adam's experience and the fruit of his sin.

This fall was reversed by Jesus Christ. The failure of the first Adam was undone by the obedience of the last Adam (as the tightly packed Rom. 5:12-21 explains). The full effects of Christ's reversal of the fall will finally emerge in the resurrection change. The whole cosmos will share in this resurrection change and will itself be renewed. Paul pictures what will happen:

> In my opinion whatever we may have to go through now is less than nothing compared with the magnificent future God has planned for us. The whole creation is on tiptoe to see the wonderful sight of the sons of God coming into their own. The world of creation cannot as yet see reality, not because it chooses to be blind, but because in God's purpose it has been so limited – yet it has been given hope. And the hope is that in the end the whole of created life will be rescued from the tyranny of change and decay, and have its share in that magnificent liberty which can only belong to the children of God! (Rom. 8:18-23, *Phillips*).

Here Paul personifies creation as 'standing on tiptoe,' stretching out its neck for a better view. Such is its eagerness for the children of God to enter into the final freedom of glory (Rom. 8:23). That entrance will mark the end of creation's own bondage to decay.

The resurrection of Jesus, the 'firstborn from the dead' (Col. 1:18), the Head of the new creation, effects the resurrection of the members of the new creation, and in turn leads to the resurrection of the entire universe. Jesus called this, significantly, the regeneration of all things (Matt. 19:28 KJV). It is the long-promised restoration that will accompany his return from heaven (Acts 3:21).

Second Peter 3:10-13 gives a more detailed picture of this cataclysmic event. Peter vividly portrays the disappearance of the heavens with a roar, the melting of the elements by fire, and the laying bare of the earth. The beauty of a glorious fireworks display set against the dark night sky pales into insignificance compared to the final divine fireworks from which a purified world will emerge in glorious splendor. Then we will see new heavens and earth that display the righteousness of God.

Behind these statements lies the great vision of Isaiah:

Behold, I will create
    new heavens and a new earth.
The former things will not be remembered,
    nor will they come to mind.
But be glad and rejoice for ever
    in what I will create...

> Never again will there be in it
>> an infant who lives but a few days,
>> or an old man who does not live out his years...

> The wolf and the lamb will feed together,
>> and the lion will eat straw like the ox,
>> but dust will be the serpent's food.
> They will neither harm nor destroy
>> on all my holy mountain

(Isa. 65:17-25).

Whatever measure of fulfillment this may already have in the church, Peter sees its consummation as still lying in the future.

The future work of God will show that he is fulfilling rather than abandoning his purposes for the earth. All things will be destroyed, but in such a way that the new world will emerge (2 Pet. 3:11). Peter had earlier used the idea of destruction in connection with the flood (2 Pet. 3:6-7). That destruction did not involve total or final annihilation but rather the cleansing of the world in a flood of judgment followed by the beginning of a new age. That is a pale illustration of the continuity there will be between the old and the new heavens and earth as well as between the present body and the resurrection body. The fire will destroy only in order to refine. The new world will come forth cleansed, changed, and splendid in its glory.

Consequently the book of Revelation pictures the new heavens and earth as a magnificent cosmos in which all that was ruined in the old is repaired and beautified. The old order will have passed away; paradise will be restored (Rev. 21:4-5). There will be access to the Tree of Life (22:2); there will be no more curse or death (21:4; 22:3); there will be undimmed fellowship with God (21:3); there will be the enjoyment of the River of Life (22:1). Best of all there will be the unhindered vision of the Lamb (22:3). God himself will have wiped every tear out of our eyes (Rev. 7:17).

Where Will You Spend Eternity?

What, then, we may ask, is the final sphere of the redeemed? Two things have sometimes led Christians to have a short-sighted answer to this question. First, some think that the Bible teaches the immortality of the soul without grasping that its central emphasis is on the resurrection of the body. This has often led Christians to envisage their final state as a completely disembodied, almost unreal, form of existence.

Second, a misreading of some passages in the book of Revelation has sometimes led to the description of the intermediate state between death and the final consummation being mistaken for the final state. Thus, quite often Christians speak (and sing) of the future life as though it were an eternally disembodied existence.

This thinking makes little sense of the biblical emphasis on the resurrection and the fact of our new bodies and no sense of the biblical teaching on the new heavens and the new earth and the fact of their existence. No, our future life will be more, not less, substantial than our present life.

Truly God's people will be in heaven, in the immediate presence of God, and 'the earth will be full of the knowledge of the LORD as the waters cover the sea' (Isa. 11:9). Heaven and earth will be as one; the new heavens and earth will be the dwelling place of man with God as well as God with man. Then, in the mystery of God's grace, there will be what our souls will have longed for: heaven on earth. The dwelling of God will be with men and he will live with them (Rev. 21:3): a heavenly earth and an earthly heaven!

But what of those who do not belong to Christ, who do not trust him as the way, the truth, and the life? This is a question that we are all, naturally, reluctant to face.

What of the Lost?

An acquaintance told us about a bereavement in his family circle. The family seems to have had no Christian convictions of any kind. Although the relative had obviously had serious health problems, the death was nevertheless unexpected. Yet, as our friend reflected on what the implications of the illness might have been, he said: 'It is probably all for the best.' That was not the appropriate time to share the thought that came immediately to mind: 'Is it?'

What is really 'all for the best': an eternity separated from God and his grace, or life with miserable health but the opportunity to repent from past sin and to turn to Christ the Savior? The New Testament is unequivocal in its teaching that there will be those who will one day go to the left hand of Christ. They will be forever lost. Their destiny is described by Christ himself in a series of vivid, terrible pictures. It is a sphere of eternal fire prepared for the devil and his angels (Matt. 25:41), a fiery, sulfurous lake (Rev. 21:8). It is a place of eternal punishment (Matt. 25:46). It is a sphere of darkness (Matt. 8:12) beyond the heavenly light (Matt. 22:13; 25:30). This is the 'blackest darkness' of which Peter and Jude speak (2 Pet. 2:17; Jude 13). It is pictured as lying outside the city of the New Jerusalem (Rev. 22:15). It is a place of weeping and gnashing of teeth – of punishment, no doubt, but apparently also of recrimination (Matt. 8:12).

Christians have never fully agreed whether such language should be understood in a literal or a meta-phorical way. John Calvin, for example, believed that these descriptions expressed God's judgments in pictorial language. After all, a sphere of fire seems incompatible with a sphere of darkness. In the final analysis, our understanding of the language of these passages is essentially a question of understanding the nature of the Bible's use of language. It is a general rule of interpretation that scriptural language should not be pressed to the point where its teaching is self-contradictory. But we must not make the mistake of thinking that what the Bible describes metaphorically is insipid reality. Hell may be described in metaphorical terms, but hell itself is not a metaphor. It is a terrible reality.

In his book *The Great Divorce* C. S. Lewis imaginatively portrays a group of visitors coming from hell to heaven, only to discover that they are so insubstantial that the solid blades of grass in heaven cut the soles of their feet. Unsuited to the life of heaven, they find it intolerable. He sees the lost as exaggerated caricatures of the people they were on earth. Just as God's children will become fully all that he has made them, so the lost will become all that they would have been apart from God's restraining grace. After all, in hell the common grace of God, which restricted the effects of sin, will be fully and finally withdrawn.

But Jesus indicates that hell involves more. God does not merely give us up to what we would become by nature. He already does that to an extent in this life (Rom. 1:24, 26, 28). No, Jesus says that hell is 'eternal fire' (Matt. 18:8; 25:42); it is 'darkness, where there will be weeping and gnashing of teeth' (Matt. 8:12). It was better never to be born than to live thus forever separated from God (cf. Matt. 26:24). Jesus teaches that there are graduations of punishment for the lost. This is the final operation of God's perfect justice. On the day of judgment some towns, like Capernaum, will have greater punishment than will Sodom and Gomorrah (Matt. 10:15; 11:20-24). Some individuals will receive fewer blows than others (Luke 12:47-48). As we have seen, however, all are punished. Justice will be perfectly administered.

The New Testament's descriptions of hell are not detailed. The truth is, no doubt, that our frail souls could no more cope with a fuller revelation of hell than they could absorb a more detailed revelation of heaven. But the biblical teaching on the reality of hell is abundant, and as clearly and dogmatically given by the Lord Jesus Christ as is his teaching on heaven.

Jesus never spoke of this with any sense of pleasure. As the Dutch-American scholar Geerhardus Vos put it,

> The subject possessed for him such a fearful reality, that, except on the most solemn and imperative occasions, he hesitated to contemplate or draw it into

the glare of open speech. It is none the less there with the ominous darkness of the untold, no unspeakable things spread over it like a semi-opaque curtain.[1]

It was, after all, Jesus himself who said:

I tell you, my friends, do not be afraid of those who kill the body and after that can do no more. But I will show you whom you should fear: Fear him who, after the killing of the body, has power to throw you into hell. Yes, I tell you, fear him (Luke 12:4-5).

These are the words of Jesus, the Savior.

A Difficulty

But how can the final state be perfectly glorious for us when we contemplate the fate of the wicked? Surely the prospect of anyone's being in hell casts a pall of deep sadness over heaven. The issue is one of psychological as well as doctrinal depth and difficulty. It is hard to think about the fate of the wicked without experiencing a sea of emotion.

One response, which has come to prominence from time to time in the church, is that the lost simply cease to exist (usually called annihilationism). Annihilationism is a position that has proved attractive to some evangelical Christians in recent years. Proponents of this view (often on the basis of the Bible's use of terms like *perish* and *second death*) say that the lost simply cease to exist. Heaven's joy will therefore not be dimmed by the knowledge that multitudes are outside in the outer darkness, forever consciously suffering

1. Geerhardus Vos, *Grace and Glory* (1922; reprint, Edinburgh: Banner of Truth Trust, 1994), 61.

the punishment of God. Since heaven will be all there is, the sense of grief that the existence of hell would produce will simply not exist.

We do not believe that the idea of annihilation is the biblical answer to these difficulties. For one thing, it does not logically provide the psychological relief its proponents often assume it does. The nonexistence of those whom we have loved deeply may *seem* to ease the thought of the pain of knowing their loss, but it does not logically or emotionally remove the pain – either now or hereafter. (See the appendix.) The absolute destruction of the lost may seem comparatively preferable to their ongoing conscious experience of separation from God, but it is not in itself a consoling thing. For what annihilationism basically teaches is that God has destroyed them. The tension remains.

Scripture itself does not address the psychological tension we feel here. Perhaps in our present sinful condition we are virtually incapable of understanding the ways in which God will resolve this issue in us and for us. But the Bible does provide us with some hints. First, it suggests that so clear will be our vision of the holiness of God and the sinfulness of man, and so full our deliverance from the presence of sin in our own hearts, that we will be able unhesitatingly to recognize God's absolute righteousness in his acts of judgment (as in Rev. 19:1-3).

Second, it may suggest by its stress on the wicked being in the outer darkness, 'outside' (Rev. 22:15), that to the citizens of the New Jerusalem, hell is but the night sky against which the city of God shines all the more brightly. Hell is that of which we will have no consciousness because we dwell in all-prevailing light.

Third, hell is the final abode of the devil and his angels, the Antichrist. It is a sphere appropriate to all those who reject Christ as the One who, while dwelling in the tiny space of a manger, filled all things. Perhaps those who fill hell see it in all its enormity, but to those who are in God's presence it is but a minute point in the distance, the dwelling place of minimized humanity (by contrast with the maximized men and women of the new heavens and earth). To it the redeemed will point and say: 'Out there, outside the city walls, the Lamb received his wounds; somewhere out there stands the Father's monument to his eternal justice.'

Even biblical revelation, however, stops short of giving us a complete answer as to what happens to the wicked. Christ has many things, surely, to say to us that we cannot yet understand. But this we do know: he has prayed for us, that we may be with him where he is, to behold him in his glory (John 17:24). In that land, he will be all the glory, for those who dwell in Jerusalem will see the King's face and be made like him.

As in all biblical teaching, we need to recognize that the New Testament underlines the importance of prioritizing. The most essential things God wants us to know are the things he reveals most frequently and clearly. Some things are not essential for us to know, and other things are simply beyond our present ability to understand. We must learn, with Moses, to absorb everything that he has revealed, but also to recognize that there are hidden things that belong only to the

Lord (Deut. 29:29). What then is important, in the light of the New Testament's teaching about heaven and hell?

It is to make sure that by faith in Christ we are assured of heaven. And then, says the apostle Peter, 'since you are looking forward to this, make every effort to be found spotless, blameless and at peace with him' (2 Pet. 3:14). That, not speculation, is our immediate task.

6

READY TO GO

We prepare for many things in our lives. We study and train for our daily work and even for our leisure activities. We plan the important events of marriage, home, and family. Some even plan dinner parties or short vacations with almost military precision. Yet few people today, even among those of us who are unreservedly Christians, prepare to die. If anything, the reverse is the case. Many of us prefer not to think or speak about the prospect of death, even though we all see it as life's one great certainty, short of the return of Christ.

There is something almost sinister about this modern conspiracy of silence; for modern it is. It is hard for us to believe that when Charles Dickens's book *The Old Curiosity Shop* was first published in a weekly serialized form, readers waited in long lines to purchase the next installment of the drawn-out deathbed scene of Little Nell. The openness of earlier generations has disappeared in ours. We are incapable of hiding the fact that death is a subject with which we cannot cope. It is discussed only in scientific terms.

A young Christian friend of ours found himself drawn into a conversation in a local store one day. On this occasion, surprisingly, the topic was death and dying. One of the shoppers, who knew something about our friend's faith, said, 'Well, Jim, we know that you wouldn't be afraid of dying.' They did not know that he suffered from a physical condition from which he might indeed die suddenly. 'No, that's true; I really am not afraid,' Jim replied. 'I would be ready to go tomorrow.' He did. The next day he was found dead. But he was prepared.

Most of us know we are not like that. Yet, if we are Christians, we sense that we ought to be better prepared. Sometimes it is only the unwelcome intrusion of a serious, perhaps even fatal, illness that stops us in our tracks. Then, for once, we begin to look at life through the proper end of the telescope – not from the perspective of the unending continuation of the certainty of death.

We have today almost lost the ability that many of our forefathers had to profit spiritually from meditation on the prospect of death. As a consequence, we are impoverished not only in the way we die but also in the way we live. How can we develop a really Christian attitude toward death? It will help us if we grasp the basic points that Scripture makes.

The True Horizon

While preparing for death and indeed anticipating it, Christians do not see their own death, or that of those they love, as the focal point of the future. Of course, an individual's death is significant. Paul, for example, was eager to die because he knew that as a result he would be 'with Christ, which is better by far,' for 'to die is gain' (Phil. 1:21, 23). But the Christians of the New Testament looked to the ultimate distant horizon: the return of Christ and the universal destruction of death that would accompany it. Seen in that light, our own death takes on a different significance altogether. Major event in our lives as it is, it is nevertheless subordinated to a yet greater event. We learn, then, to see it in its true light and context.

The Defeated Enemy

The Christian views death as a defeated enemy. On the day of Pentecost, Peter gave a vivid description of Jesus' encounter with death. Death took hold of him, and, as it were, 'pinned him down' for three days. But then death could do no more; it had exhausted all of its resources in that short time. Jesus broke its power and rose from the dead 'because it was impossible for death to keep its hold on him' (Acts 2:24). By his death Jesus was able to 'destroy him who holds the power of death – that is, the devil – and free those who all their lives were held in slavery by their fear of death' (Heb. 2:14-15).

What does this mean for us? Since Jesus was perfectly holy, neither death nor Satan had either the right or the power to overcome and imprison him. They could find no personal sin in him on which they could take a firm grip and hold him down in death. And since he died our death, in our place, he has defeated both Satan and death for us. Because we are bound to him through his Spirit's indwelling us, Satan cannot get a grip on us to hold us down in sin and death! But there is more. If Jesus bore our sin and the judgment we deserve, we will not experience that judgment. We have been justified through faith in Christ. Our status in God's presence has already been confirmed. Nothing will be able to separate us from the love of God in Jesus Christ who has provided all this for us. We need not fear.

Being with Christ

We are to set our hearts on being with Christ through death. Paul does this in Philippians 1:23 when he longs to die and to be with Christ which is, he says, 'better by far.' Notice the effect this has on him. If the Lord's will is that Paul should continue in this world, it must be because his service in the kingdom of God will be far better for others; it will be 'fruitful labor' (Phil. 1:22). Here, already, is one of the ways in which the biblical attitude toward death makes a difference throughout the whole of life.

This difference is neither accidental nor incidental. The person who sees being with Christ as far better is most likely to be motivated in his or her Christian service here and now. Those who have set their hearts on the world to come are most likely to be free from the bondage of this world and are therefore able to make an impact on it. There is something special about believers whose faith has led to this kind of love for Christ and his future presence. Love for the One who is in heaven produces a certain heavenliness about our character. Peter speaks about it in 1 Peter 1:8: 'Though you have not seen him, you love him; and even though you do not see him now, you believe in him and are filled with an inexpressible and glorious joy.'

Izaak Walton (the seventeenth-century author known best for his famous book *The Compleat Angler*) wrote of one of his contemporaries, Richard Sibbes,

Of that blessed man,
Let this just praise be given;
That heaven was in him
Before he was in heaven.

In a sense this is true of every Christian, since each one is given the gift of the heavenly Spirit of Christ. But in some it shows more clearly than in others. Those whose hearts are set on being with Christ see death as the entrance to a yet-more-glorious life that gives a clearer vision of Jesus. Such a Christian already enjoys a heavenly disposition and is prepared for the final transition.

Future Blessings

We are already united to Christ; our lives are 'hidden with Christ in God' (Col. 3:3). We should, therefore, set our hearts on the things that are above, where Christ is seated at the right hand of God, and think often and long of the blessings that will be ours.

Meditation on those blessings will transform our attitude to death and even to dying. We will begin to see it as 'going home.' Knowing that there are blessings that are kept for us will sustain us through whatever future trials we experience.

Again it is Simon Peter who captures this perfectly. He speaks about Christians being born again into a living hope through Christ's resurrection and into an inheritance in heaven. Thankfully, that inheritance is being guarded for us by God – it can never be destroyed. But, adds Peter, we are also being protected to make sure that we will obtain it. How? By God's power, yes, but also 'through faith' (1 Pet. 1:3-5). The point is this: as faith anticipates the glorious future, it is strengthened. Strengthened faith puts a spring in our step and helps us walk on our earthly pilgrimage. We thus begin to live on earth as citizens of the world to come. Faith's powers break out through us into the world in which we live.

We not only anticipate our inheritance in Christ himself, but also in and through him we will enjoy fellowship with those who are in heaven with him. Already, through faith, we 'have come to Mount Zion, to the heavenly Jerusalem ... to the church of the firstborn, whose names are written in heaven ... to the spirits of righteous men made perfect' as well as 'to Jesus the mediator of a new covenant' (Heb. 12:22-24). In heaven, this will be fully experienced. Think of the noise there will be as both the conversation and the music of this occasion fill the air. The crescendo of support that is found in the bottom of the ninth inning in the final game of a World Series will pale into insignificance and sound cacophonous by comparison with the praise on that great day of holy reunion.

We anticipate the vision of Christ. We also look forward to a great reunion with those who have already gone to be with Christ. What a prospect this is for believers! Now we have all the more reason to anticipate that great day and to live for the glory of our Savior. On that day, we are told, we will no longer see dimly, as through poor-quality glass, but face to face. In addition, we will know and understand with something of the completeness with which we have been known and understood by the Lord (1 Cor. 13:12).

Then there will be a special fulfillment of Jesus' words to Peter: 'You do not realize now what I am doing, but later you will understand' (John 13:12). We will see his providential ways in our lives – mysterious, painful, and sometimes apparently contradictory now – in all their wisdom, and we will confess with even greater worship that Christ has done all things well. Then will come the great unraveling of all the strands of his purposes. He will show us how he has woven the entire garment of history in one piece according to his perfect design. Only then will all the interconnected elements in our lives become clear.

That knowledge helps us to run onward to the world to come, and at the same time, like Paul, realize that if the Lord allows his people to be painfully separated from each other, he must have some special purpose to fulfill in and through them in the meantime (Phil. 1:23-26).

Temporary Possessions
In the light of the glory of the world to which we go, we must learn to recognize the weakness and transience of this present age. Only when our vision has been corrected by faith's grasp of the things that

are above can we have a clearer view of the true nature of the world in which we live. Only then can we see how this world overvalues the wrong things. Only then can we see poverty, loss, and sufferings, or worldly riches, success, and joy, in their proper perspective. Those who have seen the glory see the difference, just as someone who has a Stradivarius violin realizes how poor by comparison is an ordinary instrument.

The secret of dying well and entering into the world beyond is actually the same as the secret of living well here and now: having a glimpse of God's heavenly glory. Our succor when the time comes for us to taste death will be the fact that we have developed a taste for the world to come. But when we have that taste, our attitude toward both our possessions and our sufferings will change. Again Paul speaks of this attitude (notice how he is always returning to the same perspective):

> From now on those who have wives should live as if they had none; those who mourn, as if they did not; those who are happy, as if they were not; those who buy something, as if it were not theirs to keep; those who use the things of the world, as if not engrossed in them. For this world in its present form is passing away (1 Cor. 7:29-31).

Similarly our suffering and trials will be viewed in a new light. When we see them exclusively in their own new light, our difficulties and pains fill our vision. But when we place them in the light of eternal glory, their dimensions seem to change and decrease. We see that *by comparison* with the permanence and stability of what Paul calls the 'eternal weight of glory' (2 Cor. 4:17 KJV), our suffering is light and temporary.

Picture a pair of old-fashioned scales. When we put our sufferings on one of the weighing pans they seem heavy. But when glory is placed on the other weighing pan, the suffering seems light. Suffering lasts only for a while; glory will continue for ever.

The New Testament takes us a step further, however. The relationship between suffering and glory is not merely one of comparison – light and heavy weights, temporal and eternal duration – it is one of cause and effect. Suffering is the instrument that God uses to create glory. It is through the frictions and trials of life that God actually produces the graces in us that he will finally illumine in the beauty of the world to come and display in our resurrection bodies.

When one of us was young his mother had a lasting commitment to cleaning and polishing all the household items made from brass. Imagine a very small boy following his mother around the house, watching as she carefully poured out the right amount of liquid polish onto a cloth, smeared it over the brass objects, and then, after a while, returned to rub the brass vigorously to bring out its shine. The same test was always applied: 'Doing the brasses,' as we called it, was completed only when we could look at the object and see our reflection clearly. Mother was satisfied only when she could see her own face.

It is the same in the kingdom of God. He covers our lives with the polish of his providences. He creates the shine by the vigorous and often painful rubbing of trials and sufferings. He wants to see his own image beginning to emerge, and he will be content only when its full glory is reflected in the resurrection.

> For our light and momentary troubles are *achieving* for us an eternal glory that far outweighs them all. So we fix our eyes not on what is seen, but on what is unseen. For what is seen is temporary, but what is unseen is eternal (2 Cor. 4:17-18, emphasis added).

To Die Daily

There is one final aspect to the Christian's preparation for death. In view of these earlier considerations, we are to learn to die daily; to live in this world as those who do not belong to it; to live as citizens of heaven. If we die daily (1 Cor. 15:31), the day of our death will simply be the climax of all the other days in which we have yielded up our lives to the Lord.

The famous Victorian preacher C. H. Spurgeon expressed this well in one of his sermons:

> No man would find it difficult to die who died every day. He would have practiced it so often, that he would only have to die but once more; like the singer who has been through his rehearsals, and is perfect in his part, and has but to pour forth the notes once for all, and have done. Happy are they who every morning go down to Jordan's brink, and wade into the stream in fellowship with Christ, dying in the Lord's death, being crucified on his cross, and raised in his resurrection. They, when they shall climb their Pisgah, shall behold nothing but what has been long familiar to them, as they have studied the map of death ... God teach us this art, and he shall have the glory of it.[1]

This is not to say that the final death will always be easy for Christians. In the closing days of life a believer may go through a time of enormous conflict and struggle. Why should this be so?

There may be several reasons – some physical, some even satanic in character. But chiefly it is because in this life we never advance so far spiritually as to come to its end entirely uncluttered. Sometimes the love that Christ gives us for life and those who share it with us makes the leaving of them more, rather than less, difficult. In addition, we begin to realize that death, for the Christian too, is a terrible divorcing of body and soul. We do not worship our bodies; but, as the New Testament reminds us, it is natural for us to love our bodies; for they are our bodies. Moreover, for Christians these bodies have been temples of the Holy Spirit. We have endeavored to give them over, wholeheartedly and lovingly, to our Lord. We may sense, as the time of death approaches, how precious bodily life is – it is hard to relinquish such joys. Only fresh glimpses of the glory that is yet to be will sustain us at such a time.

The day of death is the great day of our divestiture when we will put off this mortal body in preparation for the great day of investiture. It is the day when we must part with all possessions, with all loved ones: wife or husband, parent or child, brother or sister, long-standing friends – all must be released from our grip. We will not, ordinarily, learn in a day the spiritual skills

---

1. C. H. Spurgeon, *Metropolitan Tabernacle Pulpit* (1887; reprint, London: Banner of Truth Trust, 1969), 14:419-20.

we need to depart this world. We die but once; but the art of dying well is one that must be learned through practice.

Sometimes, if we are to be away from home for an extended period, late on the night before we leave, we go around to each of the children's bedrooms. Watching them quietly sleeping, we stand beside their beds in silent farewell. We release from our immediate care and presence, hopefully for a short time, those we most love.

The only adequate preparation for death is to learn to do this with everything in our lives: to release our possessions from the viselike grip in which we tend to hold them, saying, 'Lord, I know you love me, and I entrust all I possess and love into your care.'

One day that releasing will take place in death. But Christ will be with us; we need not fear. In God's grace we shall be with him, and soon we shall meet again those who, with us, have trusted and loved Jesus Christ. Never again will we be separated.

While these pages were being written, in one of our families an aunt by marriage died. She was in her late eighties and had lived a long and full Christian life. On the afternoon of her death she was overheard singing quietly the words of what is probably the best-known children's hymn:

Jesus loves me! this I know
For the Bible tells me so;
Little ones to him belong;
They are weak, but he is strong.

Jesus loves me! he who died
Heaven's gates to open wide;

He will wash away my sin,
Let his little child come in.

Jesus loves me! he will stay
Close beside me all the way;
Then his little child will take
Up to heaven, for his dear sake.

Later that day, in that faith, she lay down in bed,
fell asleep, and entered heaven. With that confidence
in our hearts we too will be able to pray,

Now I lay me down to sleep,
I pray the Lord my soul to keep;
If I should die before I wake,
I pray the Lord my soul to take.

EPILOGUE

God has given Christians 'new birth into a living hope through the resurrection of Jesus Christ from the dead, and into an inheritance that can never perish, spoil, or fade.' It is 'kept in heaven' for us who 'through faith are shielded by God's power' until full salvation is ours (1 Pet. 1:3-5). But how should we live in the present day in the light of what will become ours in the last day? Paul gives us the answer:

> Since, then, you have been raised with Christ, set your heart on things above, where Christ is seated at the right hand of God. Set your minds on things above, not on earthly things. For you died, and your life is now hidden with Christ in God. When Christ, who is your life, appears, then you also will appear with him in glory.
>
> Put to death, therefore, whatever belongs to your earthly nature: sexual immorality, impurity, lust, evil desires and greed, which is idolatry. Because of these, the wrath of God is coming. You used to walk in these ways, in the life you once lived. But now you must rid yourselves of all such things as these: anger, rage,

malice, slander and filthy language from your lips. Do not lie to each other, since you have taken off your old self ... which is being renewed in knowledge in the image of its Creator. Here ... Christ is all, and is in all.

Therefore, as God's chosen people, holy and dearly loved, clothe yourselves with compassion, kindness, humility, gentleness and patience. Bear with each other and forgive whatever grievances you may have against one another. Forgive as the Lord forgave you. And over all these virtues put on love, which binds them all together in perfect unity (Col. 3:1-14).

And we, who with unveiled faces all reflect the Lord's glory, are being transformed into his likeness with ever-increasing glory (2 Cor. 3:18).

For those who experience this now, death will indeed be the gateway to a yet more glorious life!

APPENDIX
ANNIHILATION?

From time to time in the history of the church it has been suggested that those who are 'lost' experience dissolution and become completely nonexistent after death. Atheistic humanists believe that this is what happens to everyone. After all, this life is all there is. Our existence is merely physical. Death and disintegration will bring to nothing all that is.

Within the general Christian tradition, this view, known as annihilationism, has usually been held only among sects. But not always. Sometimes it has proved attractive to Christians who in other respects are committed to orthodox convictions.

Broadly speaking, these annihilationist views fall into three categories:

1. Some hold that at death the lost face God's judgment and are annihilated.
2. Others hold that at death the soul sleeps until the last judgment but then is awakened and destroyed.
3. Yet others take the view that at death the lost come

under God's judgment and consciously experience punishment and loss until the final resurrection when they will be annihilated, body and soul.

Many Christians are familiar with one or more of these views perhaps through contact with Jehovah's Witnesses or some Adventist groups that have begun in the past 200 years. But the pedigree of annihilationism stretches back beyond that.

Of particular interest here is the fact that the third view has been adopted by Christians who in other ways are widely regarded as orthodox. Indeed, they themselves would argue that the annihilation of the lost is the view that best accounts for every aspect of biblical teaching in this area. It has at least as good a claim to being truly biblical as does the traditional view. Some annihilationists argue that their view is the only biblical orthodoxy, claiming that the so-called orthodox view emerged only in the second century (in a work entitled *The Resurrection of the Dead*, which is usually attributed to Athenagoras, a Christian writer deeply influenced by the thought of the Greek philosopher Plato). It then found its real impetus in the work of the more famous theologian Tertullian. What are we to make of this?

The idea that the lost are annihilated is sometimes dismissed on the grounds that it is simply the emotionally preferable option. On occasion, annihilationists have virtually admitted this. They cannot reconcile the idea of hell with belief in the love and final glory of God. The nineteenth century Anglican F. W. Farrar probably spoke for many others when he said:

I would, here and now, and kneeling on my knees ask Him that I might die as the beasts that perish, and forever cease to be, rather than that my worst enemy should for one single year, endure the Hell described by Tertullian, or Minucius Felix, or Jonathan Edwards, or Dr Pusey, or Mr Furniss, or Mr Moody, or Mr Spurgeon.[1]

But we have not dealt adequately with a position when we have exposed its weakest and least biblical expression. In view of the explicit desire on the part of some annihilationists to be biblical, we need to consider their exposition of Scripture more carefully.

Four Arguments

The basic arguments used to support annihilation may be summarized as follows:

1. The traditional view of the eternal punishment of the lost arose from the view of Greek philosophy that the soul is immortal. If so, eternal punishment would need to last forever. But Scripture, it is argued, does not teach that we are naturally immortal. God alone is immortal (1 Tim. 6:16). God did not create us with eternal souls that sustain themselves for ever. He may therefore punish us for ever by destroying us.

2. The traditional view has assumed that the Bible's descriptions of punishment portray events that follow the resurrection. But, in fact, these

---

1. Frederic William Farrar, *Eternal Hope* (London: MacMillan Publisher Ltd., 1878), 202.

passages describe the events of the intermediate state between death and the end of the world, not the final state. To read the Bible's descriptions of punishment as though the final state were in view is to misunderstand them.

3. The traditional view misunderstands such biblical terms as *eternal*, *destruction*, and *death*, and consequently reads into the biblical text a meaning that is not there.

4. The traditional view of the existence of an eternal sphere of everlasting punishment is inconsistent with the Bible's teaching that in the end God will be truly all in all (1 Cor. 15:28). The traditional view suggests that there will for ever be a world that is somehow outside the glory of God. This places an intolerable strain on the biblical vision and limits God's glory.

What, then, are we to make of these positions?

An Immortal Soul?

Is traditional Christian teaching based on the unbiblical philosophical presupposition of the immortality of the soul? It would be foolish to deny that non-Christian philosophy influenced many of the early Christian writers; after all, it shaped the world into which and for which they interpreted the gospel. It is understandable why early writers laid emphasis on the immortality of the soul; it seemed to be a point of contact, a bridge between the gospel and non-Christians in the Greco-Roman world of the first centuries AD.

The annihilationist view, however, tends to fall into logical error here: although the idea of the soul's immortality was a useful bridge into the ancient's non-Christian world, that does not mean it came from the non-Christian world. In fact, these early theologians were simply drawing out the implications of Paul's statement in 1 Timothy 6:16: God alone is immortal. Any immortality we may have is therefore dependent on God, not independent of him. But since we were made as the image and likeness of the immortal God (Gen. 1:26-27), our being is not intended to be a temporary one.

Two elements of biblical teaching underline this: first, the resurrection of all men (Acts 24:15) makes best biblical and logical sense only on the assumption of God's commitment to the permanent character of man's being. Perhaps the most obvious weakness in the evangelical annihilationist view is that it presents God as resurrecting men only in order to annihilate them. If the real punishment for sin is annihilation, it is an odd sense of justice to resurrect the lost en route, temporarily punish them, re-embody them, and then destroy them.

Second, there is a theological principle that must always lie in the background of our thinking: how does this teaching cohere with the perfect revelation of both God and man in Christ? Evangelical annihilationists believe that Christ bore the punishment for man's sin. That, however, was an indescribable abandonment by God; it was not an annihilation. How, then, can annihilation be the divine punishment for sin if Christ did not experience it or its equivalent? In this respect Jehovah's Witnesses are more consistent; they hold that Christ dissolved into gases, ceased to exist, and was later raised up as a spirit-creature. While this logically coheres with annihilationism, it is contrary in every respect to the teaching of the New Testament.

A Misunderstanding of Scripture?

Another element in some annihilationists' reasoning is that the traditional orthodox view has been guilty of misunderstanding many New Testament passages. It has interpreted statements on future punishment as though they described the eternal state when, in fact, they speak from the standpoint and perspective of the intermediate state.

There are certain elements of truth in this criticism. Some New Testament passages that tend to be interpreted as descriptions of the final state do refer, in the first instance at least, to present rather than future realities. It is a moot point whether their application extends beyond that. For example, parts of the book of Revelation are often read as descriptions of the final state, but in fact portray the present condition of the church on earth and the intermediate state of the church in heaven.

The story of the rich man and Lazarus, recorded in Luke 16:19-31, is often expounded as though it described the final state when, in fact, it describes punishment prior to the resurrection. The rich man asks Abraham to send warnings to those who are still alive. Strictly speaking, the passage has time before the final judgment in view. Other considerations would need to be brought to bear on it to draw the conclusion that the lost are eternally conscious and eternally punished.

Other passages speak of retribution, but do not specify when it takes place. Is it not reading *into* the text (eisegesis) to hold that such retribution continues forever? We should also note, however, that an annihilationist would be equally reading into the text by suggesting that the teaching of such passages is *limited* to the intermediate state.

Some passages in the New Testament describe the suffering of the lost and clearly place it, and perpetuate it, beyond the last judgment.

Romans 2:1-16, for example, undoubtedly has the last judgment in view, rather than merely an intermediate state. It presents the enjoyment of eternal life (life forever in God's presence) as parallel with its opposite, 'wrath and anger ... trouble and distress' (vv. 8-9). This is certainly not a natural way to describe the cessation of existence.

Matthew 8:11-12 implies that weeping and gnashing of teeth follow the final judgment. That grief is set in chronological parallel to the banquet of joy that the saved experience. Again the most natural way to read this passage is to see the two (grief and joy) as continuing side by side.

Revelation 14:9-11 looks beyond the intermediate stage to the unceasing torment of those who have worshiped the beast. This is all of a piece with Revelation 20:14-15 and 21:8, where the lost share the *perpetual* suffering of the devil, the beast, and the false prophet, in the lake of burning sulfur that is of endless duration (Rev. 20:10). These are pictorial visions, but they cannot reasonably be interpreted as

115

though the *real* message being conveyed is annihilation.

It is sometimes argued that since the beast and the false prophet do not necessarily represent individuals, it would be illegitimate to build any doctrinal point out of these passages. But the devil is clearly a personal figure, and his experience of punishment is said to be both conscious ('torment') and everlasting ('for ever and ever'). Whatever the 'lake of burning sulfur' represents, it is not annihilation (Rev. 20:10). There is no discontinuity then, but continuity between the punishment experienced in the intermediate state and the perpetual loss of the final state. Indeed, there is terrible continuity.

Orthodox Christians have never completely agreed on the degree to which the Bible's descriptions of heaven and hell are to be understood literally or pictorially. Theologians like John Calvin and Jonathan Edwards held different views on this point. But there has been agreement in one area, and rightly: these passages underline the pain of lost humanity's continuing existence in separation from God.

It may be true that some passages of Scripture usually associated with the eternal state reflect only on the intermediate state; nevertheless, there is sufficient testimony to the nature of the final state to confirm that the consciousness of the lost continues. Here, too, the annihilationist position does not give the best account of the passages it cites as evidence.

Confusing the Meaning of Words?

Annihilationists argue that the orthodox view of everlasting punishment misreads the meaning of several important biblical expressions in the light of a preconceived framework. There are various illustrations of this.

One is that the word *eternal* (*aionios*) is assumed to mean 'endless' or 'everlasting' in the traditional view. Characteristically, the annihilationist here argues that *aionios* really means *aeonic*, that is, 'belonging to the age to come' without reference to its duration. *Eternal* refers to quality, not longevity. Thus, 'eternal punishment' (Matt. 25:46) does not mean eternally enduring punishment, but 'the punishment of the age to come.' There is no necessary reference to endless consciousness. Again, 'everlasting destruction' (2 Thess. 1:9) does not refer to a destroying that goes on and on, but to that which is appropriate to the age to come. It is the destruction (i.e., annihilation), not the destroying, that is lasting. But this interpretation faces an insuperable objection. The term *aionios* is used in the New Testament in the context of the biblical distinction between the present age and the age to come. Within that theological framework, 'the age to come' is *by definition* endless, endlessness being an essential element in its quality.

A second illustration is that many annihilationists argue that the nouns that occur in conjunction with 'eternal' indicate not an *action* that is endless, but a *result* that is enduring.

Thus, when Hebrews speaks of 'eternal salvation' (5:9) and 'eternal redemption' (9:12), in view is a permanent state, not an ongoing process. In Mark 3:29, 'eternal sin' is not sin that goes on and on but sin whose implications are eternal.

It should be noticed that here 'eternal' is allowed a significance that annihilationists employing the first argument have denied it. Be that as it may, this line of thought is especially relevant in such phrases as: 'eternal judgment' (Heb. 6:2), 'endless punishment' (Matt. 25:46), and 'endless destruction' (2 Thess. 1:9). What is eternal here is not the judging, the punishing, or the destroying, but the implications of a once-for-all judgment, punishment, and destruction. The destruction takes place in a moment, but it is eternal in the sense that its implications last forever. The second death then is real death – final annihilation.

Thus stated, the argument appears to have considerable force. But we must not confuse the possible meaning of a phrase with its actual meaning in a specific context.

What is death? It is cessation. Annihilationists therefore argue that the second death of which Scripture speaks implies annihilation. The traditional view has tended to emphasize the adjective *eternal*. But this, it is claimed, is to miss the force of the noun, *death*. In Scripture, however, death is the opposite of life in communion, whether with man or God. It is not the opposite of existence. Death is not the cessation of consciousness, but it is separation from fellowship with God. This was already clear in Genesis 2 and 3 where the state of death was not the end of existence but the end of life in fellowship. The Old Testament scholar Franz Delitzsch put it well when he wrote:

'Death and annihilation in Scripture are not by any means coincident ideas.'[2]

What then of the ideas of *perishing* and *destruction*? Again our understanding of these terms must be dictated by their biblical use. Their normal use does not imply the cessation of existence altogether, so much as the disintegration of a previously constituted condition or state. Several illustrations will demonstrate this point.

Matthew 9:17: Men do not put new wine into old wineskins, or they will be destroyed ('ruined'). Here, what is destroyed is not the existence of the wineskins, but their ability to function as intended.

Luke 9:24: The man who loses (i.e., destroys) his life will find it. Here again the idea of total annihilation of the individual is clearly absent.

Hebrews 2:14: By his death Jesus destroyed the devil. This clearly does not imply the annihilation of the devil. He was not annihilated by the death of Christ. John actually tells us the whole world lies in Satan's power (1 John 5:19). As we have seen, Revelation 20:10 assumes that he will not be annihilated in the future. Thus, when the author of Hebrews speaks of the devil's destruction he is thinking of the destruction of his power in a particular sphere. Once again *destroy* does not mean *annihilate*.

Romans 6:6 (KJV) confirms this: Paul speaks of the body of sin as being destroyed. The *New*

---

2. Franz Delitzsch, *A System of Biblical Psychology*, trans. R. E. Walter (Edinburgh: T and T Clark, 1899), 475.

International Version clarifies the point by employing the translation 'rendered powerless.'

2 Thessalonians 1:7-9 is of special interest in this connection. It speaks of being 'punished with everlasting destruction and shut out from the presence of the Lord.' But if 'destruction' means complete and total annihilation: (1) the adjective 'everlasting' serves no function whatsoever, and (2) 'shut out from the presence of the Lord' loses its force, since the phrase naturally implies ongoing conscious existence. Paul is speaking here of the destruction that consists in being excluded from the presence of God (probably using the form of speech known as hendiadys, in which one thought is expressed by two ideas). Instead of implying cessation of existence, therefore, the biblical terminology actually underlines its continuation.

Some annihilationists argue that the illustrative language used in Mark 9:47-48 and its parallels implies annihilation. There Jesus speaks of 'hell, where 'their worm does not die, and the fire is not quenched.'' The background to these words is found in Isaiah 66:24 with its gruesome picture of judgment in terms of flies laying eggs in festering corpses; the eggs become maggots and eat away the rotting flesh. In addition there is an unquenchable fire that destroys. The traditional exegesis has assumed, often admittedly without arguing the case, that this describes everlasting torment. In fact, annihilationists argue, it is absolute destruction that is in view; after all, fire consumes.

But, again, this overweights the text. The annihilationist argument depend on a very literalistic interpretation of this picture. If we were to take the statement literally like this, we would need to recognize that the point of the statement is that these worms do not die and the fire is not quenched. But if so, the fodder and the fuel must continue. Thus, even when the annihilationist view pushes the metaphor beyond its intended limits, it does not support the annihilationist exegesis.

An Imperfect Conclusion?

The traditional view of hell, some annihilationists argue, suggests that there will always be something 'contrary to God's will.' This is more than an emotional difficulty in accepting the existence of an everlasting hell – it is a theological obstacle. By contrast, the total destruction of the wicked is more consistent with God's final reign over all things.

On the traditional understanding, there will always be an aspect of the created order that does not conform to God. Augustine put it starkly:

> After the resurrection, however, when the final judgment has been completed, there shall be two kingdoms, each with its own distinct boundaries, the one Christ's, the other the devil's; the one consisting of the good, the other of the bad ... the former shall live truly and happily in eternal life, the latter shall drag a miserable existence in eternal death without the power of dying; for the life and the death shall both be without end.[3]

Annihilationists argue that this everlasting dualism places an intolerable strain on the biblical vision that envisages all things being brought together in Christ and under his lordship and supremacy (Eph. 1:9-10; Col. 1:18-20). It also seems inconsistent with Paul's grand expectation of God's being all in all (1 Cor. 15:24, 28). This surely requires that there must be nothing left that stands over against God. In the final world there can be no lasting darkness.

Annihilationism also seems to provide an answer to our psychological as well as theological difficulties and questions: how can I rejoice in the presence of God when I know there are others – whom I have loved, even come to love because of the grace of God himself has put in my heart – who are not in heaven, but are forever suffering the pain of hell? Here we reach one of the outer boundaries of revelation, and we must think and speak with modesty and humility. But is the annihilationist view really a more satisfactory and coherent account of what Scripture teaches?

Given certain assumptions, annihilationism may seem to be the better resolution of these difficulties. But again several things should be noted. First, we do not find all the loose ends tied up in this way in Scripture itself. Instead we find another emphasis. In the biblical visions of heaven, the saints are portrayed as rejoicing in the judgment of God on his enemies. His holiness is terrible when it punishes sin. But his

---

3. Augustine, "Enchiridion," trans. J. F. Shaw, in P. Schaff, ed., *Select Library of the Nicene and Post-Nicene Fathers*, first series (1890; reprint, Grand Rapids: Eerdmans, 1956), 3:273.

punishment is also absolutely holy, expressing the glory of his justice.

This does not mean that God's people find malicious pleasure in the suffering of others. But they do recognize God's justice. No hint is given that the effects of God's righteous judgment constitute a psychological problem in heaven.

We cannot understand that fully. We feel we cannot trust our *fallen* emotions to rejoice like this now. Indeed, we cannot, because 'now is the time of God's favor, now is the day of salvation' in which we urge our relatives and friends 'not to receive God's grace in vain' (2 Cor. 6:1-2). But this should not blind us to the startling fact that we will recognize God's absolute justice on the day in which it is righteously expressed against the full measure of man's sin.

Furthermore, it would be a mistake to imagine that those who reject the idea of eternal punishment because it is psychologically difficult to accept could be fully comforted by being told: 'You need not feel thus, for those who are lost have been utterly annihilated by their Creator.' On either position (the orthodox or the annihilationist view), there will be what now seems to us the most agonizing loss. Only universalism (the teaching that all, without exception, will be saved) would ease that pain, and that, clearly, was not the teaching of either Jesus or the apostles.

Second, the New Testament affirms that every knee will bow to Christ and every tongue will confess that he is Lord, to the glory of God the Father (Phil. 2:10-11). Whether in grace or in justice, all things will manifest his unsullied glory. The orthodox view may seem to suggest that there will be a dark blot on the last and future world, but only in the future will we also understand that even this 'black hole' in the final universe displays the divine glory.

Third, Scripture tells us that there is an outside to the walls of the New Jerusalem (Rev. 22:15). There is an outer darkness, where, because it is both outside and dark, there will be weeping and gnashing of teeth. As with the other mysteries of our faith, our minds and emotions cannot yet grasp the full meaning of this. We can, however, entrust the ordering of even these things to the perfect wisdom and righteousness of our God.

The issues here are not simple, nor is everything about God's final judgments crystal clear. In fact, these judgments are terrible, and in many ways it is well they are in some respects opaque and beyond our understanding. With Augustine we have to say: 'I see the depth, I cannot reach the bottom.'[4] Here, as elsewhere, biblical revelation leaves us gazing into a light that has the capacity to blind us. Some secrets of our faith are resolved only in the mind and knowledge of God, not – at least not yet – in ours.

At such points as these we must learn to bow in humble and adoring wonder before the glory of the Lord. But as we do so, we need to bear in mind that while 'the secret things belong to the Lord our God ... the things revealed belong to us ...' (Deut. 29:29). The truth we do know and grasp serves a practical purpose in our lives. Consequently, our conclusions about this theme cannot be of merely academic interest.

---

4. Quoted in J. Calvin, *Institutes of the Christian Religion*, III.23.5.

Most evangelical Christians believe the doctrine of everlasting punishment. This is what the lost will receive when they stand before the judgment seat of Christ; this is what is due them for the things done while in the body (2 Cor. 5:10). But in view of this teaching we must ask:

Do I appreciate my salvation in the light of what Christ delivers me from?

Do I appreciate what it is that Christ did for me when he became sin and a curse in order that I might receive the righteousness and the blessing of God?

Do I appreciate what it means that instead of wrath I will receive a crown of righteousness?

Do I have a biblical view of my neighbors, knowing that I, too, must appear before the judgment seat of Christ? Do I try to persuade them to seek and find salvation in Christ?

The doctrine of the last things must never be reduced merely to the level of intellectual, theological jigsaw puzzles. If we do not feel the weight and see the implications of the issues, we are not fit to discuss them.

THE OTHER SIDE OF THE GOOD NEWS

CONTEMPORARY CHALLENGES
TO JESUS' TEACHING ON HELL

LARRY DIXON

The Other Side of the Good News

Contemporary Challenges to Jesus' Teaching on Hell

Larry Dixon

Larry Dixon examines current theories and encourages you to take the Bible's teaching on hell as seriously as Jesus did. If he came to give us the Good News then we don't want people to spend eternity on the other side of the Good News.

Three alternative views to the traditional doctrine of hell are examined; universalism, annihilationism and post-mortem conversion. In a thought-provoking final chapter Larry summarises how different views affect our interaction with non-Christians and the extent of our freedom to hold different views.

'Larry Dixon is refreshing! His courage in dealing with the "hard truth" of the much ignored doctrine of hell is to be commended – a "must read" for every believer.'

Steve Brown, KeyLife Network

'...capably defends the church's historic position on hell... respectfully interacts with opponents and writes in a manner that is at once attractive, passionate and accessible to ordinary believers.'

Robert Peterson, Covenant Theological Seminary

'In a climate where universalism is very fashionable, Dr. Dixon stands forthrightly in support of the traditional orthodox doctrine of endless conscious punishment.'

Roger Nicole, Reformed Theological Seminary

Larry Dixon is Professor of Systematic Theology at Columbia International University, South Carolina.

ISBN 1–85792–804–0

Christian Focus Publications

publishes books for all ages. Our mission statement:

STAYING FAITHFUL

In dependence upon God we seek to help make His infallible Word, the Bible, relevant. Our aim is to ensure that the Lord Jesus Christ is presented as the only hope to obtain forgiveness of sin, live a useful life and look forward to heaven with Him.

REACHING OUT

Christ's last command requires us to reach out to our world with His gospel. We seek to help fulfill that by publishing books that point people towards Jesus and help them develop a Christ-like maturity. We aim to equip all levels of readers for life, work, ministry and mission.

Books in our adult range are published in three imprints.

Christian Focus contains popular works including biographies, commentaries, basic doctrine and Christian living. Our children's books are also published in this imprint.

Mentor focuses on books written at a level suitable for Bible College and seminary students, pastors, and other serious readers. The imprint includes commentaries, doctrinal studies, examination of current issues and church history.

Christian Heritage contains classic writings from the past.

Christian Focus Publications, Ltd
Geanies House, Fearn, Ross-shire,
IV20 1TW, Scotland, United Kingdom
info@christianfocus.com
www.christianfocus.com